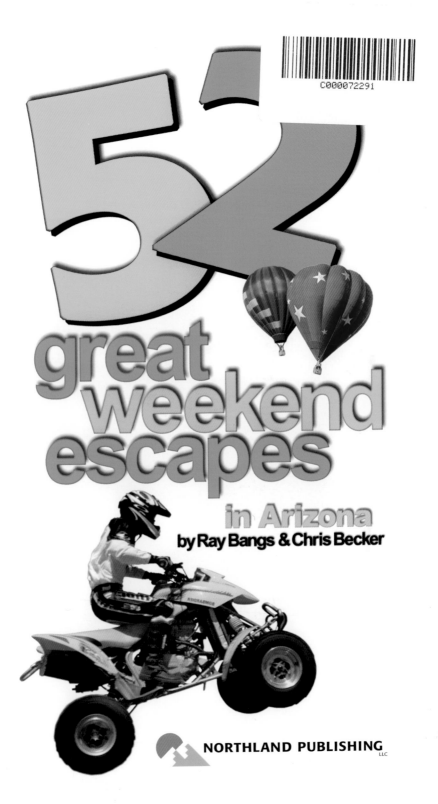

52 great weekend escapes

in Arizona

by Ray Bangs & Chris Becker

NORTHLAND PUBLISHING LLC

www.northlandpub.com

Cover: Kayaking (Photograph by Peter Zwagerman), Ballooning
(Courtesy of Greater Phoenix Convention and Visitors Bureau), Super-Karting (Photograph by Rick Scuteri),
Horseback Riding (Courtesy of Rancho de Los Caballeros), Fishing (Photograph by Dave Foster)
Title Page: Quad (Photograph by Ray Bangs)
Page 6: Cactus (Photograph by Ray Bangs)
Page 52: Tubing (Courtesy of Mesa Convention and Visitors Bureau)
Page 100: Leaves (Photograph by Klaus Kranz)
Page 150: Skiing (Courtesy of Arizona Office of Tourism)
Back Cover: Hummer Tours (Courtesy of Hummer Adventure Tours),
Jet Skiing (Courtesy of Lake Havasu Tourism), Flying (Courtesy of Fighter Combat International)

Special thanks to Danielle Becker for her help in creating the maps.

Composed in the United States of America
Printed in Hong Kong

Edited by Tammy Gales
Designed by Lanie Schwichtenberg
Production supervised by Donna Boyd

FIRST IMPRESSION 2002
ISBN 0-87358-800-2

02 03 04 05 06   5 4 3 2 1

Library of Congress Cataloging-in-Publication Data Pending

Northland Publishing is not affiliated with the www.52weekendescapes.com
website, and is not responsible for its contents or maintenance.

The information in this book has been carefully checked and to the best of our knowledge is accurate.
However, details are subject to change, and Northland Publishing and the authors cannot be held responsible
for such changes, or for errors or omissions. Assessments of outfitters, hotels, and activities are based on the authors'
subjective opinions, which do not necessarily reflect the publisher's opinion. The publisher and the authors
cannot be held responsible for any consequences arising from the use of this book.

Editor's Note: At press time, all BLM (Bureau of Land Management) websites were temporarily frozen
due to pending court cases. We have left these websites in the book
with hopes of them coming back online.

I wish to dedicate this book to
my family and friends, and especially to
my sister Katie, who helped me dream up
these 52 weekend escapes over
a couple of icy cervezas.

—RAY BANGS

This book is dedicated to
my wife Danielle, who was not my wife
when this project started and might not ever
have been if it went on much longer.
I love you.

—CHRIS BECKER

Table of Contents

Photograph by Dave Foster

Introduction

"Let's do something this weekend."
"Well… What do you want to do?"
"I don't know. We could go to a movie?"
"Um… I don't know. That's what we did last weekend."
"There's got to be something else to do."
"Must be… I don't know."

Before we started exploring, we had this conversation over and over, and there's no doubt we weren't the only ones. Every weekend we struggled to think of a new and exciting idea, maybe an unusual place to visit or a different activity to try, only to end up ordering a pizza and watching the game of the week. Our first problem, looking back to those days, was that researching everything felt too much like work. As exciting as it was to look at the colorful pictures and maps of our potential destinations, planning the trip from scratch took a big bite out of our leisure time. And really, as much as we knew a weekend escape was exactly what we needed, the Saturday and Sunday dozing-on-the-couch routine was too easy. We were content with waiting and watching, so we never really stepped from the sidelines to charge headlong into the game.

52 Great Weekend Escapes in Arizona is designed to cut these problems off at the pass and help you to order up your own slice of the adventure pie. All the homework (most of it, anyway) has already been done for you. You'll be amazed at what's out there! With this book in hand, you've got a prime chance to discover a new piece of Arizona, as well as something new about yourself. So look through your choices, make a few phone calls, and then go do something new and adventurous. It doesn't get any easier than this!

How To Use This Guide

The first step to using this guide is to select the type of activity you are interested in. Start by reading through the wealth of exciting options and picking out a couple to try. Each escape is broken down into the following six sections:

Season

The weekend escapes are organized by their most optimal season. Keep in mind that you can enjoy many of these activities any time of the year. Heed warnings about temperature extremes, though, especially in the summer, and always remember to take plenty of water. Also be aware that the monsoon season of late summer and early fall creates dangerous flash floods that can make adventures such as hiking in Paria Canyon deadly. Be sure to check with the respective management agencies and outfitters for weather updates, forecasts, and current conditions.

Difficulty

Please be advised that the levels of difficulty assigned to these escapes are based only on our opinions and those of the outfitters. The difficulty levels should not be taken as an indication that everyone may be able to perform each activity. It is your responsibility, as the weekend warrior, to decide what kind of escape you are physically and mentally able to handle. Be aware that it is always a good idea to prepare your body and mind for all the adventures offered in this book, and that some activities require more effort and training.

The ratings can vary greatly depending on how you choose to pursue the activity. For example, riding a mountain bike around the local park may be easy, but riding technical downhill singletrack in the McDowell Mountains requires an entirely different level of fitness and expertise. Likewise, whitewater kayaking the Upper Salt River, sky-diving, hang gliding, and various other escapes are not for beginners. In most cases, we provide contact information of outfitters or guides that can help you learn the basics of an activity. It is up to you to decide if you need more preparation for an activity. Just make sure to choose an escape that will suit your skills and abilities, then practice and physically prepare yourself in order to make the experience more rewarding.

As far as the ratings go, an easy adventure is one that most average people can do, with less regard to age or fitness level. Many are family-oriented activities and often involve guided tours or seminars, tourist activities, or relaxing leisure destinations. Some require moderate amounts of easy hiking, but nothing that will bother most people with an average level of fitness. Minimal technical skills may be required. For example, tubing the Salt River or even a weekend rafting trip in the Grand Canyon do not require gold medalist swimming skills, but if an emergency arises, you'll need to keep a clear head and doggie-paddle to stay afloat. Similarly, driving too big of an RV might not be appealing to some. While you should certainly not try to do anything you cannot handle, the simple fact is that because these are all active vacations, under the worst circumstances, things can go wrong. The easy rating signifies that the probability of things going wrong is lower.

A medium rating means that there is usually some prior skill required to perform the activity, or that a moderate level of fitness is required. Some of them can be family activities, though there are fewer here than in the easy category. For example, renting a Harley is a medium-difficulty adventure because no one will rent you a $15,000 motor-cycle if you've never ridden anything bigger than a ten-speed. A weekend at the Shangri La Ranch is rated medium because not everyone has the guts to "let it all hang out" at a nudist resort. On the other hand, mountain biking is a medium-level activity because it requires some fitness and endurance to complete the trail, as does playing paintball or hiking Peralta Canyon. In general, expect to prepare more for these medium level adventures, or have the required equipment (or the knowledge of how to use the required equipment) before you take them on.

Difficult adventures are tests of skill, endurance, and courage that aren't right for everyone, but will reward those who seek them out. They require a peak level of fitness, as well as previous active, outdoor experience. They are meant for those people who feel proficient and at home in the wild outdoors and want to test themselves even further against more extreme conditions. Some are just plain tough, like rock climbing or moun-taineering, while others, such as SCUBA diving or paragliding, can be dangerous if you don't pay attention to what you're doing. Several combine more demanding activities with weather extremes, and the risk of injury is generally increased. Some of these difficult activities may be experienced on a limited basis to whet your appetite and entice you to further pursue the sport. So while every weekend escape in this book in every difficulty rating can be taken to the nth degree, never try an activity that clearly exceeds your capabilities, especially without proper training and preparation.

We mentioned physical conditioning before, but it bears repeating. In trying any of these escapes, your adventure will be more rewarding if you are physically prepared for it. It is no fun to be sore all week after a demanding weekend. If you are, you're less likely to look back at the experience with fond memories, and therefore, less likely to take a similar challenge in the future. Working with a health professional to prepare a proper regimen of aerobic exercise and strength training is a great way to both get in shape for your trip and generally improve the quality of your life. You can also simulate your adventure on a smaller scale and practice near your home. Your local hiking trail may not be quite as rugged as parts of the Superstition Wilderness Area or the Grand Canyon, but it can certainly help to prepare your legs for the terrain there. It comes down to this: the healthier your body is, the less of a factor physical work becomes in your escape, and the more you can enjoy your surroundings.

While you're preparing your body, don't neglect your mental plan, especially for the most challenging of our escapes. Although your goal is to relax and have fun, intense concentration is often necessary while whitewater kayaking, rock climbing, paragliding, and in any other endeavor demanding close attention to detail. Prepare your mind for problems that may arise. We all hope for the best situation, but the possibility of the worst is something you should be ready for, especially when the activity takes on an element of danger due to treacherous conditions. By being mentally alert and prepared when you go, you'll be better equipped to handle whatever your adventure might throw at you.

Finally, don't be discouraged by the risks of these activities. The better prepared you are to accept and deal with the inherent risk of challenging yourself, often in an unfamiliar environment, the more you will gain from your adventures.

Price

Quite often, prices for each escape will vary across a somewhat broad range, allowing for your individual preferences. The cost for your adventure will depend on what level of adventure you're looking to take and especially what kind of accommodations you choose. The only factor not included in this price range is the cost of travel. With destinations scattered all over the state, we've left it up to you to factor in the cost of travel between your home and the adventure.

But do not fret over the cash. The nice thing about this little book is that many of the outfitters here offer discounts. Just refer to the coupons at the back of the book for the full array and be sure to check out www.52weekendescapes.com for additional coupons and updates. Armed with a little forethought and this money-saving guide, you should be able to experience many of these adventures with minimal financial difficulty.

Description

The descriptions will let you know what each activity entails, what to expect when you go, and how to prepare for the experience. We've also provided a little more inside information whenever possible—ideas, suggestions, even warnings to keep you informed about aspects of the adventure you may not have thought about. So choose the adventures that sound appealing to you, make a few phone calls, prepare yourself, and follow our advice (and your outfitter's) about what to do once you're there, and you'll have a great weekend.

Maps and Directions

The maps and directions lead you to the start of your adventure, whether it is the park entrance, trailhead, parking lot, or even the café where an outfitter often meets clients. This resource should help eliminate the need for piles and piles of maps and atlases. Use the maps to get a general idea of where your escape is located, and then follow the written directions to the start of the adventure.

Outfitters and Contact Information

We know that the hardest part about doing something active is the planning; so to make it easier on you, we have listed tour operators, outfitters, and related contact information at the end of each escape. And, just in case you want to read up on your chosen escape before you go, we have also included an additional reading list. It's quite understandable if your first skydive takes just a little extra convincing!

All groups mentioned in this book are listed simply because they are considered among the best in what they offer. No listing fees were charged, so no company bought their way in. The included providers have proven themselves to hundreds, and often even thousands of active travelers. Each of the outfitters offers an enjoyable experience complete with excitement, education, relaxation, discovery, and fun. They all have great track records for safety and excellent customer service. The guides and trip leaders are pleasant and polite, as well as technically skilled, in order to ensure a safe and stress-free outdoor experience. Your outfitter will inform you of any special equipment, training, or skills necessary. They will let you know what it takes to be adequately prepared—both physically and mentally.

When we chose outfitters and tour operators for this book, cost was taken into account, but not as heavily as the actual value of the escape. You might find other companies that may be less expensive or less experienced than some of the ones included here. If you decide to go with them, you may be sacrificing a fun vacation, a lifetime of memories, or maybe even your safety, all for the sake of saving a few dollars. We found the best of the best, the people who are going to deliver the most bang for the buck, rather than a cut-rate experience at a cut-rate price. Many of these first-class operations have agreed to provide a discount to owners of this book, though none of them had to do so to be included here. (Just being the best was enough!) In the back of the book you will find details on the savings with their corresponding coupons. In most cases, the money you can save on just one adventure will more than cover the cost of purchasing *52 Great Weekend Escapes in Arizona*.

Make Your Adventure Memorable

So you've taken the plunge—you've scheduled a weekend of hiking, or soaring, or camping, and now you're anxiously waiting for the minute you can be on your way. As this will be something new and special, you'll want to make sure that your adventure stays fresh in your mind for a long time to come. Here are a few suggestions to make the memories last well into your future:

Take Lots of Pictures—We can't stress this enough. Photos are the best way to tote the one-of-a-kind sights Arizona offers home with you, whether that home is in Tacoma or Tucson. If all you can muster is the eight bucks required to buy a throwaway camera, then do it; if you can, though, you might want to invest in a 35 mm or digital camera to record all of your adventures. The more pictures you take, the better you'll get at it, and if you learn how to use a camera correctly, you'll be more able to capture the splendor and sights around you. Eventually, the great pictures become as much a part of your adventuring as the activity itself, and you get the added bonus of a photo album that is exciting to return to years after the escape is over. Best yet, showing your kids and even your grandkids that photo of you hang gliding or on a Grand Canyon mule ride helps ensure you can pass your newfound adventurous spirit on to future generations.

Keep a Journal—Especially on hikes and drives, this method of capturing the moment is easy and intensely personal. Our state offers many inspirational landscapes, from the painted red rocks of Sedona, to the majestic Grand Canyon, to the rugged beauty of the Sonoran desert. Writing about the incredible sights, describing your feelings, and detailing your thoughts will allow you to appreciate the experience even more. Keep an ongoing travel journal, and you'll have interesting reading a week, a year, or ten years later.

Take Family and Friends Along—All of these activities can easily be enjoyed by groups of people, and in most cases, are more fun with family and friends. Learning to kayak or SCUBA dive alone is not nearly as enjoyable as learning with someone else, preferably one with whom you can share the activity after the initial training is done. And if you find that you want to pursue the adventure further by becoming more proficient or turning it into a regular pastime, you'll have a partner who will enjoy traveling that road with you.

Join a Club—There are clubs and organizations for every kind of outdoor activity, from skydiving to skiing to spelunking. And they are by no means limited to Arizona; if you happen to take up rock climbing on your Arizona vacation, you'll still find an interested community back in Wichita, Atlanta, or just about anywhere. In our Internet-connected world, it's not hard at all to find these clubs and join them, or to at least attend some of their meetings. If any of the adventures here really get you going, the best way to repeat the experience is with others as interested in it as you are. The clubs are a great way to meet those people. At the very least, these organizations can direct you towards your next adventure, and you may also find yourself making a new group of lifelong friends.

Buy Equipment—As you start your weekend adventures, you'll find that most outfitters will provide the major equipment needed for an escape. But if you find an activity that you plan to regularly pursue, the best way to improve your skills is to invest in your own set of gear, personalized to your specific body type, skill level, etc. Some of the gear can get pretty expensive, but if you talk to some folks who are already involved in the activity (try the clubs mentioned above, or the outfitter you choose), they will be able to direct you to the best stores and used equipment networks. Once you do know what you're looking for, the options are even better. Flea markets, yard sales, and Internet auction websites are often three great places to find cheap, quality gear.

Get to Know Your Outfitter—Any person who makes a living doing some outdoor activity is worth staying in touch with, especially if you're planning on staying involved. If you've had a great experience, tell them so and use them the next time you're planning a similar escape. Many of Arizona's outfitters even cross-specialize in multiple activities, and the folks who took you kayaking may be the same ones who can give you a screaming deal on a fantastic hiking adventure. At the very least, they might have good ideas about who to call for a different escape, even if they don't provide the service themselves.

Arizona boasts enough adventure to satisfy everyone. It's truly a shame to visit, or worse yet, to live in Arizona and not search out these great experiences. *52 Great Weekend Escapes in Arizona* is meant to provide you with the information to get you well on your way to becoming a modern-day explorer, appreciating our amazing natural surroundings, and discovering exactly what adventure is all about. Use this guide as your starting point, and soon you'll be forging your own path, creating new escapes, and sharing them with people who, like you, are looking to get into the game. So chose an escape, prepare yourself, stay safe, and have fun exploring Arizona!

Spring

Sonoran Desert Hummer Tour

Operation Codename Pretty Flowers

Easy
$100-$250

You've just flown into Phoenix, and now that you're on the ground you start to notice the desert around you in all of its sun-blasted, barren splendor. "Amazing," you think, "but all this seems a bit boring." You think back to Yellowstone, Glacier, or Rocky Mountain National Parks—places where the landscapes surround and overwhelm your senses with height and density—and wonder what this place might have to offer you. Or, maybe you've been living in Arizona for a year, or four, or twenty. You've been to the Grand Canyon and Sedona, been hiking a few times, maybe even bought a mountain bike. But every time you drive across the vast spaces of open Sonoran countryside, you find yourself thinking, "What's out there? It looks like a whole lot of nothing." You couldn't be more wrong.

The Sonoran desert that surrounds Phoenix is the Arizona that most people from

Courtesy of Hummer Adventure Tours

around the world know. It is the hot, scrubby desert that graces a million postcards, and outside of the Grand Canyon, it is our state's most recognizable natural feature. Though Arizona's environment is amazingly diverse, it is this dry ocean that defines the state to most folks.

Whether you are a visitor or a native Arizonan, this expanse is one of the best places to start your Arizona adventuring, simply because like Arizona itself, the desert seems to be one thing and ends up being quite another. This is especially true

in the springtime when the desert flowers are in full bloom and the temperature is not yet punishing. This time of year is the best season to experience the Sonoran Desert, and the best way to do it is in the king-daddy of all adventure vehicles, the Hummer.

Forget pedaling over stones or hauling a forty-pound pack on your back under the blazing sun. The Hummer is not just something movie stars drive; the original purpose

of this vehicle when it was first built for the U.S. military was for it to go anywhere, under any conditions. It can scale a 22-inch vertical rock ledge or climb up a 60% grade. It can plow through 30 inches of water, mud, or snow. Thanks to 37-inch tires and almost a foot-and-a-half of ground clearance, the Hummer makes a whole new kind of off-roading possible—and the Sonoran desert demands just that kind of vehicular athleticism.

SONORAN DESERT

Salt River
Indian Community

Four Peaks
Wilderness

Roosevelt Lake

Shea Blvd

Saguaro Lake

87

Canyon Lake

Apache Lake

Tortilla Flat

Superstition
Wilderness

60

To Mesa (Phoenix)

Courtesy of Hummer Adventure Tours

The reason is that this landscape is not the wasted, featureless land you see when you're looking at it from a plane, or speeding past it on the freeway. It is a dynamic, living region, covered in spots by boulders and buttes and in others by saguaro forests. It is by no means flat or dead. In the summer, the Sonoran desert comes closest to the popular conception of it; the sun falls like an anvil out of the sky, and the environment becomes a dangerous and fatal place. Countless recreational hikers and mountain bikers regularly suffer heat injuries and even die in the scorching summer desert. The spring, as we mentioned before, is quite a different story.

Rain is still sparse, so the flowers race each other to bloom. First, the smaller flowers such as the catchfly and the fairy dusters present themselves; then the little shrubs appear; and finally, the cacti, the living symbol of Arizona's deserts, flower in full glory. As the plants bloom, animals that are dependent on the plants' bounty slowly show themselves, too. This includes every creature from the morning doves and curve-billed thrashers to the cottontails and the coyotes. The animals use this time for mating and birthing, which gives the desert spring an even greater feeling of life and vitality.

But, putting nature aside for a moment, let's get back to the Hummer.

Most of the Hummer tour companies in Phoenix have a range of adventures, from day-long expeditions with lots of sightseeing to shorter, adrenaline-packed extreme drives through areas it's tough to walk through, let alone drive through. They usually last from four to nine hours depending on where you go and what you're doing. The extreme tours tend to be shorter, since gas goes faster when you're grinding over large objects. Popular destinations include the Tonto National Forest, the trails around Saguaro Lake, and the rest of the Four Peaks Wilderness Area. The unique land features like canyons, cactus forests, and mountains rising from the desert are proof that this landscape has as much diversity as any region in the country. As your trip progresses, you will see new flora and fauna at every possible turn.

The beauty of seeing this amazing splendor in a Hummer is that your guide can literally take you anywhere, and is generally happy to do so. Granted, there are designated areas and trails that Hummer tours will stick to so as not to trample on too much of the Sonoran's natural beauty and balance. For the most part, though, your untrained eye won't even be able to tell that you're on any kind of "track" seeing as how the track still has giant rocks in it and runs up and down canyon walls.

A cool bonus is that some of the Hummer tour companies will let you drive the truck once you're out in the wilderness. The experience is as incredible as driving slowly can get. This vehicle is truly one-of-a-kind, and worthy of all the press it gets. Behind the wheel, you'll feel mighty and invincible. Be sure to ask about these driving options during your initial calls. The companies offering this perk will tell you up front while you're discussing your trip.

Knowing what you're in for is the most important part of preparing for your Hummer adventure. If you want the extreme experience, be ready to get thrown around a little bit. The Hummers will keep you as comfortable as possible, but let's face it—driving over foot-high obstacles and careening down into washes is going to buck the truck a little bit. If you have chronic back problems or a similar ailment, stick to the gentler packages. The same advice goes for those of you with kids; if they are the kind of tykes who jump out of oak trees on homemade bungee cords, then they should be okay on the bumpier rides, but younger children might be uncomfortable. Just remember to ask the right questions of your tour company—are their Hummers air-conditioned, are beverages included, do I get to drive—and you will have the best possible time.

Taking in the desert through a Hummer's windshield is perhaps the best way to start a life of adventuring in Arizona, whether your adventures take place over the course of a week or a lifetime. It will familiarize you with the Sonoran landscape and plant a seed inside you, one that will draw you back again and again to this most unlikely, yet enjoyable, environment.

Directions

Depending on the Hummer tour company you go with, you will either meet at their headquarters or get picked up from your home or hotel. When you call for reservations, they will let you know.

Outfitters

Desert Dog Hummer Adventures (see coupon pg 201), Fountain Hills, AZ
    480/837-3966, www.azadventures.com/humadv
Hummer Adventure Tours (see coupon pg 201), Chandler, AZ
    602/743-7369, www.hummertour.com
Stellar Adventures, Inc. (see coupon pg 201), Scottsdale, AZ
    602/402-0584, www.stellaradventures.com

For More Information

AM General, www.amgmil.com
Hummer, www.hummer.com

Recommended Reading

Green, Michael. *Hummer: The Next Generation.*
    Osceola, WI: Motorbooks International, 1995.
Phillips, Steven. *A Natural History of the Sonoran Desert.*
    Berkeley, CA: University of California Press, 1999.
Quinn, Meg. *Wildflowers of the Desert Southwest.*
    Tucson, AZ: Rio Nuevo Publishers, 2000.

Photograph by Dave Foster

2 Lee's Ferry
The Art of Fly Fishing

Easy
$0-$500

If fly fishing is an art, then the 15-mile stretch of the Colorado River at Lee's Ferry is one of the world's greatest canvases. The crimson cliffs and sparkling clear river provide the backdrop as you paint away with the fly rod. And then, all of a sudden, out of the depths comes a tugging on your line that can be as subtle as a gentle caress or as hard hitting as a jackhammer.

Located below Glen Canyon Dam, Lee's Ferry is perhaps the most rewarding fly fishing trip you can take. Besides the incredible beauty of the canyon, healthy populations of Rainbow and Cutthroat trout provide plenty of pole-bending action. The fish average 12 to 18 inches, but 20-inch fish and bigger are not uncommon. It can be a frustrating experience, though, because even though the monster-sized trophies are so easily seen, they are more finicky, growing big by not being so easily fooled. Catch-and-release is highly encouraged, but a strict daily bag limit of only two trout under 16 inches helps ensure great fishing for generations to come.

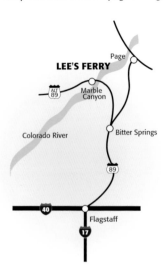

The water temperature stays at a constant 45° F, making Lee's Ferry a year-round tailwater. The only problem with the winter months is the colder air temperatures; but with warm, layered clothing, insulated waders, and a thermos of hot coffee or cocoa, you will stay quite comfortable. Much of the good fishing upriver consists of wading around the gravel bars and islands; however, this area is only accessible by boat. Renting a jet boat is one option, but going with a guide is a much better one. Not only do they know the fishing hotspots, but they also know where the shallow water hazards are along the way. An outboard propeller motor is suitable, but keep a sharp watch for obstacles. A spare propeller, extra cotter pins, and the necessary tools should be on your checklist. If you choose to walk instead, there is more than a mile of shoreline up and downriver of the boat launch. Although the scenery is spectacular throughout the area, a boat ride will allow you to see more of it, and most people agree that the fishing upriver is better.

Fly fishing Lee's Ferry is generally not for first-timers, but only because the fish receive moderately heavy pressure and there is usually an abundant food supply of scuds and midges. The clear water means you can see the fish, but they can also see you! Because of this fact, your technique is crucial, adding an extra incentive to hire a guide. It may cost more, but after only an hour or so, your casting skills will be considerably improved and your presentation will be much more realistic. The guides are also well stocked with all the best fly patterns. Good fly choices include a selection of size 16-22 midges in red, brown, and black. (Many guides are especially fond of the zebra patterns.) Cinnamon, pink, and rusty-orange colored scuds in a variety of sizes up to size 12 are also popular. Just keeping up with the names of all the popular dry flies is overwhelming, so be sure to ask at the fly shops to see what's working. Fly tying is such a complex hobby

Photograph by Dave Foster

that there are even flies specifically designed for the fish here, such as the "Lee's Ferry Wooly Bugger." If fly fishing is not your preferred angling technique, spinning rods definitely work too, but fishing with live bait is prohibited and keep in mind that all flies and lures must be barbless. Barbless hooks ease the stress when releasing a fish, and despite some reluctant critics, they are just as effective.

Many people mistakenly believe that Lee's Ferry is a big water fishing area calling for hefty rods and long casts, but with the abundance of shallow edges and gravel bars, it almost seems like you are in a small wilderness stream. A 4 or 5 weight rod works well. The casts don't need to be very long, because the most popular fly fishing method is to use a downstream drift. You just cast well upstream of that huge trout you see, and let the current take your fly. If you're lucky and the fly looks real enough, you will be reeling one in shortly. The fishing goes in streaks, often fluctuating with the river flows and water levels. When the water is lower, the scuds get marooned on land and the sun dries them out. When the water levels rise again, they fill the streams and the trout have more than adequate food so your fly has less chance of being picked. Weekend water levels are usually lower and the fishing is excellent, however, every day has great potential. Rarely will you ever get "skunked" and not catch a fish.

Most fishermen and women arrive at the river by dawn, but they return to the docks shortly after lunch. The river is often less crowded later in the day and it can even appear desolate in the evenings. As a bonus for staying longer, you will be treated to the late afternoon sun playing tricks on your eyes as colors bounce off the canyon walls. More recently, people are choosing the increasingly popular option of combining fly fishing with a round of golf at the Lake Powell National Golf Course in Page. Several guides at the various outfitters specialize in this and have even arranged discounted greens fees with fishing packages. Even after a scenic round on the links, you can still enjoy six or more hours on the river.

A bonus to being at Lee's Ferry and in the Vermillion Cliffs area is that over two dozen endangered California Condors have recently been reintroduced. They are the first to fly outside of California in over 70 years. This is a real success story, with more California Condors now flying wild in Arizona than there were in the whole world only 20 years ago. Courtship behavior is even being recorded, and the scientists tracking the birds are optimistic that breeding in the wild will occur in 2002 or 2003. So be sure to at least occasionally glance upwards, with their wings spanning over nine feet, they're hard to miss!

Accommodations in the area range from campgrounds to rustic lodges to luxury hotels. Lee's Ferry Campground, located one mile below the boat ramp, has 50 first-come, first-served sites with flush toilets and fire rings. Additional campsites with similar facilities are located at several points upriver and are accessible only by boat. Marble Canyon Lodge, Vermillion Cliffs Lodge, and Cliff Dwellers Lodge are all within 10 miles of Lee's Ferry. More sleeping options and full services can be found approximately 45 minutes away in Page.

Lee's Ferry is truly a world-class fly fishing destination. Imagine telling your story about playing a round of golf, reeling in many hefty trout, spotting the largest and rarest North American bird, and finally, being the last boat off the river. This adventure is definitely worth at least one weekend. To ensure the best experience, enlist the support of your local fly shop to learn the techniques and decipher the lingo before you go. After a trip to Lee's Ferry, you will definitely find yourself in love with the art of fly fishing.

Directions

Lee's Ferry is located in north central Arizona, 15 miles below Glen Canyon Dam and Lake Powell. From the north, go through Page and drive south on Hwy 89 to Bitter Springs (23 miles). Turn north on Hwy 89A and go 14 miles to Navajo Bridge. The Lee's Ferry junction is on the right, approximately 300 yards west of the bridge. If you are traveling from the south, follow Hwy 89 from Flagstaff and turn north on 89A at Bitter Springs.

Outfitters

Glen Canyon Anglers (see coupon pg 201), 877/369-5563, www.glencanyonanglers.com
Lee's Ferry Anglers, 800/962-9755, www.leesferry.com
Marble Canyon Guides (see coupon pg 201), 800/533-7339, www.mcg-leesferry.com

For More Information

Glen Canyon National Recreation Area, 928/608-6404, www.nps.gov/glca

Recommended Reading

Foster, Dave. *Dave Foster's Guide to Fly Fishing Lee's Ferry.*
    Sisters, OR: No Nonsense Books, 2001.
Reilly, P.T. *Lee's Ferry: From Mormon Crossing to National Park.*
    Logan, UT: Utah State University Press, 1999.

3 Meteorite Hunting

Hidden Secrets from the Heavens

Easy
$0–$500

Meteorite hunting brings together the work of archeologists and astronomers, with a little nod to *x-Files*-watching UFO aficionados. Imagine searching the beautiful badlands of Arizona for pieces of distant worlds, and the feeling you'll get when you find that rare object that began its existence tens of millions of miles away from here, on another planet long since gone. Or, on a more material level, imagine finding a two-ounce nugget of gold worth five hundred dollars.

These are the kinds of rewards that lead people to the world of meteorite hunting and its more wealth-driven cousin, gold prospecting. Hunting for gold has been a popular pursuit across the West since the mid 1800s, and in more recent years, it has experienced a resurgence in popularity with the advent of more technically advanced metal detectors. These detectors allow rock hunters to probe under the soil up to eighteen inches deep, without going through the old time-consuming method of panning the earth and separating the good stuff from the plain old dirt.

As a result of the newer time-saving methods, the idea of going out into the desert and searching for gold is more of a hobby than a pursuit exclusively meant for grizzled prospector types with no family or, well, prospects. In fact, one doesn't have to spend a

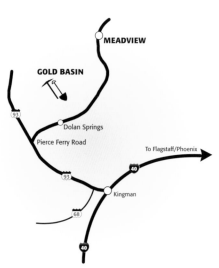

month in the lonesome valley to find their just rewards. In 1999, a hobbyist prospector named Jim Salada found a three-ounce chunk of gold in Arizona's Gold Basin, and folks who hunt the Basin regularly often find multiple smaller chunks. It takes patience, but with the right guidance and a steady hand, you might find yourself yelling with joy across the plain just like those old-school grizzled guys.

Meteorites are a more lofty pursuit, as they do offer some small monetary value (Arizona State's Center for Meteorite Studies is always on the lookout for more quality specimens), but they generally appeal to a sense of wonder rather than the wallet. They are, after all, a piece of the universe and owning one creates a connection between yourself and the cosmos. Arizona, being relatively dry, wide, and open, is a perfect depository for these heavenly stones, and the state abounds with them.

Meteorites are pieces of space material, and generally, they are planets, comets, or asteroids, smashed apart by collisions with other spaceborne objects. They can be metallic (usually iron) or rocky, and most of them are pretty small. Occasionally, a big meteorite plunges through the atmosphere and smacks into the Earth, creating a massive crater and a lot of grief for the inhabitants who live around the impact. Winslow's Meteor Crater, for example, is almost a mile in diameter and 600 feet deep, and it threw little pieces of space debris about twelve miles in every direction. Bigger chunks are more valuable, but the little guys around two to six grams are pretty easy to find in "strewn

fields," which are areas where meteors exploded before hitting the ground and the small fragments dispersed across tens of miles.

Gold Basin, located about forty-five miles north of Kingman and one of the state's best known strewn fields, is a great area for collecting both gold nuggets and extraterrestrial minerals. It is a wide open desert, dotted with sparse scrub brush, and it is covered with millions of tiny rocks and pebbles. These small pieces of ground cover, along with the layers that hide right underneath them, are interspersed with valuable gold and meteorites; the idea is to use metal detectors to separate the good finds from the plain old desert rocks.

Granted, if you're a beginner, you won't have a detector of your own to hunt with, nor will you really know what you're looking for. That's why on your first weekend trip you should tag along with some people who not only provide you with the knowledge you lack, but the equipment you need. One such outfit is the Lifestyle Store, a California-based operation that primarily serves as an outdoor equipment supplier. Once a year, though, they expand their services by taking a group of beginning prospectors out into Gold Basin and teaching the newcomers the basics of searching for meteorites. They provide equipment rental, which includes the use of more specialized equipment like deep seeking metal detectors. The workshops last three days and allow the participants a chance to not only hone their searching skills, but to socialize with other people who share the same interests. The Lifestyle Store provides sample meteorites for examination before you start your hunt, as well as good instruction as to the best ways to search the

Courtesy of The Lifestyle Store

Basin. Lots of food and drinks are included with the seminars that are presented by meteorite and gold hunting experts.

In all, the outing is a great opportunity to get out into the Arizona wilderness and engage in a quietly exciting and very rewarding activity. The country around you is beautiful in its barrenness, and the people who you are adventuring with are interested in showing you how to best enjoy your outing. There's more to the adventure than hunting, too; you can choose to camp out (provided you bring your own equipment), and make the weekend into a complete outdoor experience. For you domesticated types, never fear—you can choose to stay in one of the nearby hotels if tents are a little too far into the "roughing it" category. Even RVers are welcome; Meadview RV Park is very close to the Lifestyle Store camp area, and it provides reasonable rates and amenities to those who want them.

This is an adventure for fun and profit, the kind of activity that pays for itself if you're lucky and come up with some gold. Even if you don't, though, you can look forward to sharing good company, learning a new skill, and experiencing a weekend in the desert with all of its Zen-like beauty. And if you happen to discover a rock from Mars with tiny fossilized creatures in it, well…Area 51 is due north, at least that's what the feds tell us. They might be interested in your little discovery.

Directions

To get to the Meadview RV Park and the Lifestyle Store campsite take I-40 west to Kingman (you can reach I-40 from Phoenix by taking I-17 north.) From Kingman go west on Hwy 93 towards Las Vegas. On 93 turn north at mile post 42 onto Pierce Ferry Road and drive to mile post 34. Pierce Ferry Road is county highway 25 and is paved the entire length. The park is located a couple of hundred yards off the pavement. When arranging the Lifestyle Store tour, be sure to mention you will be meeting the group at the campsite.

Outfitters

The Lifestyle Store, 800/900-6463, www.lifestylestore.com

For More Information

Meadview Chamber of Commerce, 928/564-2425, www.meadview.info
Meadview RV Park, 888/775-2662, www.rv-park.com
Meteor Crater, 800/289-5898, www.meteorcrater.com

Recommended Reading

Angier, Bradford. *Looking for Gold: The Modern Prospector's Handbook.*
    Mechanicsburg, PA: Stackpole Books, 1982.
Chronic, Halka. *Roadside Geology of Arizona (Roadside Geology Series).*
    Missoula, MT: Mountain Press Publishing Company, 1986.
Norton, Richard O., Norton, Dorothy, & Marvin, Ursula B. *Rocks from Space: Meteorites and Meteorite Hunters.* Missoula, MT: Mountain Press Publishing Company, 1998.

4 Tombstone & Tucson Studios

Legends of the West and Hollywood in Arizona

It doesn't take long to notice that this little book you've been perusing doesn't include any theme parks, miniature golf courses, carnivals, or more "amusement-oriented" attractions. This fact is by design; riding a roller coaster doesn't qualify as much of an adventure, as it is easily repeatable and pretty much standard vacationer material. For the same reason, we've avoided much of the pop culture Arizona has to offer. There are plenty of places to eat great food, see a good show, and hear a good band; if you check the local entertainment paper, you'll find out where they are.

But Hollywood...Hollywood is something different. There is something about our culture that celebrates the cinema and pushes movies into the realm of national art. Movies are bigger than local music or theater, and they bring our culture together. The Western film in particular represents a distinctly American character that your basic comedy or action flick just does not capture. Like the Blues, the Western is an American forum, just as the idea of the West is an American phenomenon.

The fusion of Hollywood's attraction and the Western mystique comes together in Arizona's own monument to the movie industry, Old Tucson Studios. Founded in 1939, the Studios have played host to over 300 films, TV shows, and commercials, all of which seek out the Western spirit that only a few places still manage to capture.

The Studios are fully functional, meaning that filming is often going on. And since the Studios always remain open, you have a rare chance to step behind the scenes and see what goes on during movie production. Call in advance to see what productions are happening while you're there, because you might get to see anything from a small-scale

Courtesy of Metro Tucson Convention and Visitors Bureau

Courtesy of Metro Tucson Convention and Visitors Bureau

commercial shoot to a top-of-the-line production like *Tombstone* or *Wild Wild West*, both of which were partly shot using the Tucson Studios lots and props.

When you head out there, be sure to check out the great entertainment. Unique shows of all kinds move through them, from comedy "medicine shows" to the more intense gunfight re-enactments. Above all, these productions are fairly original and often very good, even for adults; the stunt exhibitions in particular are well worth seeing. These demonstrations give insight into how you can throw a guy through a window or knock him off a three-story building without him getting hurt—or worse. It is probably the most interesting exhibit on the lot, since you can learn a great deal about how stunts work as well as be entertained by them. If you're lucky, the stunt crew will work you into the act and let you participate in a stage brawl or a quick-draw gunfighting contest.

The Studios are ideal for family entertainment, as all of the fun is meant for all ages. However, there is one exception—the Iron Door Mine ride is a bit on the scary side for little ones, so make sure they know what's coming if you let them ride. Other rides include stagecoach jaunts (complete with shootouts), horseback trail rides, and a ride area for the kids. You will also find a nice array of Western-style food and shopping available. Whether you decide to visit with the kids or some friends, remember that you might be picked to brawl with the stuntmen or get "rained on" by quack rainmakers. Be ready for anything!

If country music is your thing, then you will want to keep an ear out for who's playing at the Studios, too. Many national acts swing through Tucson on their way across the country; just visit the Old Tucson Studios website or call them for a detailed schedule of upcoming events. Again, these shows are simply pleasant additions to your Tucson Studios experience; the main idea is to experience Hollywood first-hand, and take in the magic of the movies.

After spending one day in the artificial West of Tucson Studios, you should probably take a step back and see for yourself just where the Wild West mystique was born. Though much of the original lawlessness is gone, the sites that make up the mythology of the West are still intact and quite accessible. Drive out about seventy miles to Tombstone, the "town that refuses to die," and you'll see the reality and legend that made the West such a popular subject for Hollywood films.

Tombstone was the location of the most famous gunfight in Western history—the showdown at the OK Corral between Wyatt Earp, Doc Holliday, and their allies on one side, and the infamous Clanton/McLaury boys on the other. The Corral is preserved just as it was on that day in 1881; walk through and learn what led to the shootout, as well as the mechanics of how it happened. It is as close as American history gets to mythology, and that hallowed ground is right here in Arizona.

You are not going to Tombstone just to take in the Corral, though. The town is filled with the legendary West, from the Boot Hill graves marking the final beds of America's most famous outlaws, to the groups of actors dedicated to bringing the West to life every day. Head over to the Tombstone Courthouse State Historical Park and learn all about the sordid history of the town from well-versed research specialists. The town lives and breathes its wild history, nurturing it for everyone who takes an interest in the West.

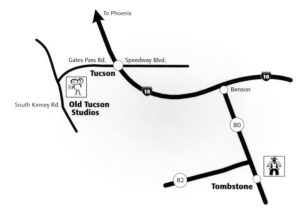

While both the Studios and Tombstone are, individually, great day outings, combining them creates a wonderful weekend of Hollywood glitz and Wild West charm. The price is right too. Entrance to the Old Tucson Studios for a family of four costs just under $50 and Tombstone is free except for the postcards. Where you want to stay is up to you and your budget, but Tucson offers the gamut of accommodations from tent and RV parks to luxury hotels. Contact the Tombstone Chamber of Commerce for lodging options; ask about the Flamingo House, the Buford House B&B, and Curly Bill's, all of which are Tombstone landmarks.

And, if this rich history hasn't inspired you enough, get a fresh perspective on the Western mystique by asking one of the many foreign visitors what it is about the American West that drew them here. Sometimes it is hard for those of us living in a place to realize what is so special about it. Talk to our visitors and find out, especially if you're an Arizona native. Then maybe you'll rediscover what brought you here in the first place.

Directions

To get to the Old Tucson Studios from Phoenix take I-10 to Tucson and exit on Speedway Boulevard west, which turns into Gates Pass Road. Continue through Saguaro National Park, until you come to Kinney Road. Turn left on Kinney and head south. You will see signs for the Studios. To get to Tombstone from Tucson, follow I-10 east. When you reach Benson, take state Route 80 south.

For More Information

Old Tucson Studios, 201 S. Kinney Road, Tucson, AZ , 520/883-0100
www.oldtucson.com
Tombstone Chamber of Commerce, 888/457-3929, www.tombstone.org
Tucson Convention & Visitors Bureau, 520/624-1817, www.tucsoncvb.com

Recommended Reading

Burns, Walter. *Tombstone: An Iliad of the Southwest.*
Albuquerque, NM: University of New Mexico Press, 1999.
Dollar, Tom. *Tucson to Tombstone: A Guide to Southeastern Arizona.*
Phoenix, AZ: Arizona Highways, 1996.
Murray, John. *Cinema Southwest: An Illustrated Guide to the Movies and Their Locations.* Flagstaff, AZ: Northland Publishing, 2000.

Golf Getaway

There's Gold in Them Hills

Easy
$100-$500

Sometimes you just want a break from your job and the routines of everyday life. When work time creeps into our limited playtime, our overall existence becomes more stress-filled and less rewarding. It is time for an escape! For many, the certainly interesting and sometimes too challenging game of golf is an ideal way to relieve stress.

There are hundreds of golf courses in Arizona ranging from the basic, most inexpensive municipal layout to the very exclusive, private country clubs. Just about every budget can find a place to play, and usually, there will be dozens of choices within minutes of your home or hotel. If golf is a rewarding pastime for you, try getting away for a weekend just to play golf and lots of it. For two or three days, you can forget about the most recent crisis at work or the major project you have coming up. It's time to just relax and tee it up…again and again and again.

If you need a good recommendation, Gold Canyon Golf Resort is a great place to spend your weekend. Gold Canyon's two spectacular courses winding around the foothills of the legendary Superstition Mountains provide more than ample incentive to take this weekend adventure. Be forewarned though, these courses are not necessarily for beginners, because depending on your choice of tee boxes, even pros find the layouts demanding. However, one of the reasons golf can be so great is because no matter what your ability level is, the game itself is intrinsically challenging.

Gold Canyon Golf Resort is located approximately forty-five minutes east of Phoenix. During the drive, the landscape gets more spectacular with each passing mile. When you arrive, you might even think for a moment that you are in the French Riviera with all the bleached white casitas speckling the landscape. Upon closer inspection, you will discover that their southwestern style and luxury compete with even the most elegant and well-known resorts. The Gold Canyon Golf Resort has recently spent millions of dollars on their accommodations in order to match their two top-notch golf courses, and the changes have transformed the resort into a prime destination and world-class facility.

Many of the spacious casitas offer amenities such as jumbo-sized Jacuzzis, romantic fireplaces, and even private patios with scenic views of the backyard mountains. The fabrics and furnishings in each casita welcome you with their southwestern charm.

Your first round at the championship Dinosaur Mountain course will leave you breathless. The desert air is clean and clear with blue skies stretching as far as you can see, and the horizon is marked by the distinct peaks of the Superstition Mountains. Pristine desert washes that are abundant with wildlife remind you that golf courses are still natural habitats for many creatures. Jackrabbits, coyotes, javelinas, and roadrunners, all quite common at Gold Canyon, are a small sampling of the wildlife that help shape Arizona's character. The surprising number of native birds can almost be distracting at times as they whistle their relaxing chants. This staggering natural beauty is complemented by perfectly manicured fairways hugging the natural

contours of the land, which the talented staff keeps conditioned well above par year round.

The Dinosaur Mountain course consistently contends for the #1 Public Golf Course in Arizona rankings. With the number of incredible courses in the state, even making the top ten is a very prestigious honor. A round of golf at the Dinosaur Mountain course will certainly be visually entertaining with its lush, undulating fairways surrounded by wide-reaching views of the Sonoran desert. Luckily, the invention of the golf cart makes the dramatic elevation changes feasible, but there will even be times when the little electric motor struggles. When you can hit your nine-iron over 200 yards, you know elevation is a big factor. The round can also provide other entertainment, usually to your playing partners. Dinosaur Mountain, played from the farthest-back tees, known in golf lingo as the "tips," is one of the toughest courses in Arizona. For most golfers, the only birdies you see will be the ones chirping away while you play.

Sidewinder is the second course at Gold Canyon Golf Resort and is underrated simply because Dinosaur Mountain is right next to it. The greens fees are roughly half the price, but the quality is not at all cut-rate. Sidewinder is somewhat easier than Dinosaur, but the challenge is of course, relative. Sidewinder runs through the area's natural arroyos and dry creek beds at the foot of Dinosaur Mountain. Several of the tee shots start a little higher in elevation, but they do not feature as many of the sometimes outrageous elevation changes like its "big brother." Prickly pear cactus, cholla, and palo verde trees can be seen throughout the course, serving as reminder that you are still in the desert.

If your game is not quite up to par, the quality instruction of the Resort Golf School can help shave a few strokes off your game. Southwest Section PGA Teacher of the Year, Scott Sackett, leads the program. Whether you are a beginner or carry a single-digit

Courtesy of Mesa Convention and Visitors Bureau, Photograph by Gary Johnson

handicap, spending a day with the top-notch instructors at Gold Canyon will significantly improve your game.

Although golf is the highlight, Gold Canyon Golf Resort offers all the amenities of a great destination. The swimming pool and tennis courts give you more active options on-site, while the nearby Lost Dutchman State Park provides miles of hiking trails. Apache Trail Tours will pick you up right at the resort in one of their jeeps and guide you around the rugged terrain of the Superstition Mountains. Those interested in this fabled area's rich mining history will find the nearby Goldfield Ghost Town and Mine Tours fascinating. Slightly farther away is Salt River Canyon, known as the "Junior Grand Canyon" and home of the Dolly Steamboat, where you can relax on a scenic ride aboard a steam-powered replica of an old-fashioned sternwheeler paddleboat.

Gold Canyon Golf Resort offers numerous options for stay and play weekends. You can easily squeeze in two rounds a day, or start with 18 and then try out a few of the other activities. However you choose to spend your weekend in the Superstitions, great golf, excellent service, and a relaxing atmosphere will make you feel right at home. You'll hear plenty of stories about gold in the hills around the resort, but the real treasure is the great golfing. Don't be too frustrated about your scores though. While the courses can be challenging, don't forget that the main fun of golf is just the experience of playing.

Directions

From Phoenix follow US-60 east to Kings Ranch Road (watch for the signs). Turn left to the resort.

For More Information

Apache Trail Tours (see coupon pg 201), 480/982-7661, www.apachetrailtours.com
Dolly Steamboat (see coupon pg 201), 480/827-9144, www.dollysteamboat.com
Gold Canyon Golf Resort (see coupon pg 201), 6100 S. Kings Ranch Rd.
    Gold Canyon, AZ 85218, 800/624-6445, www.gcgr.com
Goldfield Ghost Town and Mine Tours, 480/983-0333, www.goldfieldghosttown.com

Recommended Reading

Huffman, Bill. *Arizona's Greatest Golf Courses.*
    Flagstaff, AZ: Northland Publishing, 2000.

6 Mountain Biking Arizona

Running Room for the Aluminum Steed

**Medium
$0-$100**

Along with hiking, mountain biking is one of the Big Two Arizona outdoor activities. It stands as one of the most popular, pervasive, and addictive wilderness sports there is. Some people are weekend dabblers looking for gentle hills and soft tracks to dig their tires into; it grabs others by the throat and never lets go. Some take it easy on flat terrain, while others kamikaze off 10-foot high boulders. These lives belong to Arizona's mountain bikers. If you're one of them, you probably already recognize yourself fitting one of the descriptions above. If you aren't, then maybe it's time you learned something about yourself and decide which of these pedal pushers you are.

Arizona has more to offer bikers than just about any other state in the country, and

Photograph by Paul Beakley

it attracts a good number of them. One reason is our general lack of rainfall. This fact makes the muddy impassable trails that haunt other states seldom a problem here. Our bikers are also lucky in that they don't have to worry about much competition for trail space with hikers or other bikers. In Arizona, we have countless numbers of marked trails as well as areas for backcountry biking, so with just a little effort you can easily find yourself alone for miles.

The work is in finding these places, the lesser-known routes that don't attract the kind of traffic that landmark locations like Mount Elden near Flagstaff or South Mountain in Phoenix do. Of course, these locations attract bikers because they are good; if you're coming from out of state to bike Arizona's best-known and most popular trails, take the time to visit the big names. But if you're a native looking for something new and different, or a visitor trying to delve deeper into Arizona's wealth of biking runs, just peruse the following list and hit as many of these locations as you can.

Pima and Dynamite Routes, Phoenix: This network of trails just outside of Phoenix provides over

one hundred miles of single track riding for bikers of all skill levels. It is a beautiful example of Sonoran desert wilderness, and perfectly located for Phoenix residents or tourists using the city as a base of operations. The trails are unmarked, so keep your bearings by keeping the power lines in view (an old jeep road runs right under them.) There are two warnings, though. First, watch out for rattlesnakes, and second, keep an eye out for the ATV crowd. There are a lot of motorized riders out here, so pay attention—their bikes are bigger than yours!

Cathedral Rock, Sedona: This is a nice little trail that passes right by Oak Creek, where you can take a dip and wash off the trail dirt. It is for riders of moderate skill, as the trail hits some fairly difficult technical points. The effort is worth it, though, when you gaze out at the incredible desert scenery that surrounds you.

Sunrise Ski Resort, McNary: During the off-season, this ski area offers all-day, weekend lift tickets for mountain bikers for only $15 apiece, creating a downhill lover's paradise. Imagine spending the whole day on steep, varying runs without having to pedal! It is possible here, and the best part is that the place is mostly deserted. It is well worth the drive, as you can ride nearly all day and never cover the same ground twice.

Photograph by Paul Beakley

John Krein Trail, Tucson: This is a tough ride in the Tucson area that climbs to a 360-degree view of the Tucson Mountains. It's not for beginners, and with the scorching desert heat it should be avoided during the summer. You may encounter some hikers at the beginning of the trail, but don't fear—once you reach the Krein Trail proper, you should be alone with the few two-wheeled adventurers who join you.

Robber's Roost, Sedona: This is a 20-mile out-and-back trail, taking you through the beautiful red sand hills surrounding Sedona. The highlight is the namesake hideout carved into the butte, where cattle rustlers and horse thieves once kept watch over their herds. There are amazing views as you get up the butte, which provide further proof of Sedona's unique beauty.

Sample these trails over the course of several weekends and you'll get a nice cross-section of Arizona's biking resources. You'll experience the desert and the forest, and all without running into crowds of hikers or having to pay for a pricey guided expedition. Just throw the bike on the rack, follow the map, and go. But bear in mind that summer is not the time to bike in Arizona without taking all necessary precautions. Bring lots of water and leave early. In the spring you should be okay, but watch the forecast for early heat waves and thunderstorms.

Of course, the adventure does not have to stop there; in fact, you shouldn't stop with this little smorgasbord of trails. Thousands of trails pepper the Arizona countryside, so wherever you find yourself, simply visit the local bike shop to get a better feel for what opportunities surround you. If you don't own your own bike yet and are not sure if mountain biking is for you, dozens of stores also offer rentals for reasonable rates. Arizona mountain biking shows no signs of slowing down in popularity, so you might as well jump on the bandwagon and join the fat-tire frenzy.

Directions

Pima and Dynamite, from Phoenix: Take 101 north to Pima and go to Dynamite Road. Park on the south corner, and follow the power lines north across Dynamite Rd. to the trailheads. Cathedral Rock, from Phoenix: Take I-17 north to Hwy 179. Follow 179 west to Oak Creek. Park near the Circle K where the trail starts. Sunrise Ski Resort, from Phoenix: Take State Hwy 87 north to Payson. From Payson, take State Hwy 260 east to Show Low. At Show Low, keep on 260 through Pinetop and McNary to State Hwy 273. Turn right on 273; Sunrise Park Lodge is four miles down, and the ski area is three miles

Courtesy of Way Out West Treks and Tours

past the lodge. John Krein Trail, from Tucson: Take Speedway Boulevard west of town. It will change to West Anklam Road, and then to Gates Pass Road when it goes over Gates Pass. Continue west on Gates Pass Road and turn left when it intersects Kinney Road. Watch for parking area K9 on the left, around a mile and a half from the intersection. Robber's Roost, from Sedona: Head west out of town on 89 towards Cottonwood. After about six miles, you will see Forest Service Rd. 525 on the right. Turn off here, park the car, and ride.

Outfitters

Arizona Off-Road Adventures (see coupon pg 203), Tucson, AZ
520/822-9830, www.azora.com
Arizona Outback Adventures (see coupon pg 203), Scottsdale, AZ
480/945-2881, www.azoutbackadventures.com
Arizona White-Knuckle Adventures (see coupon pg 203), Scottsdale, AZ
866/342-9669, www.arizona-adventures.com
Way Out West Treks and Tours, 520/825-4590, www.wowtnt.com

For More Information

International Mountain Biking Association, 888/442-4622, www.imba.com
Mountain Bike Association of Arizona, 602/351-7430, www.mbaa.net
Sunrise Ski Resort, McNary, AZ, 800/772-766, www.sunriseskipark.com

Recommended Reading

Beakley, Paul. *Outside America: Mountain Bike America—Arizona.*
Guilford, CT: Globe Pequot Press, 2001.
Bicycling Magazine. "Mountain Bike Magazine's Complete Guide to Mountain Biking Skills: Expert Tips on Conquering Curves, Corners, Dips, Descents, Hills, Water Hazards, and Other All-Terrain Challenges." New York, NY: Rodale Press, 1996.
Cosmic Ray. *Arizona Mountain Bike Trail Guide: Fat Tire Tales & Trails.*
Flagstaff, AZ: New Millennium, 2000.

7 Off-Road Adventures

Unleashing the Grocery-Getter

Medium
$0–$100

Do you own a truck or an SUV? Ask yourself how many times you've driven it off the pavement. If that sporty new Xterra or Wrangler is just used as your transportation to work and as a grocery-getter on the weekends, you're missing out on the vehicle's built-in ruggedness. Yes, it was actually designed to go off the road! If you have a 4WD and have not escaped the asphalt yet, it's time to try something new and justify having spent the extra bucks. Arizona has hundreds of off-highway options ranging from graded gravel suitable for any passenger car to smooth slickrock impossible for the typical SUV or truck to negotiate. Once you get off the pavement, though, a whole new world of adventure awaits.

First, a word of caution—SUVs and trucks may be rugged, but they are not invincible. They cannot go everywhere and you definitely should not just blaze your own trail across the desert. Proper planning is always important, because there are few things worse than running out of fuel 50 miles from the nearest major road. If you forget to bring water and food, you could find yourself in serious trouble. Additionally, if you don't know how to change a tire, the spare won't do much good. Off-roading is a social activity, so the more the merrier, and safer. All vehicles are machines that can break down, so having a

Photograph by Ray Bangs

couple other trucks along can help if you need a tow, or in a worse case, when you need a ride home. Plus, going with others is almost always more fun.

Before setting out on your off-road expedition, make sure your vehicle is ready and stocked up with several essentials. A strong battery, a spare tire (or two), extra fan belts, good hoses, basic tools, and a reserve of gasoline and oil are important; extra radiator water is also a good idea. A small shovel, heavy-duty yank or tow strap, jack and base plate, jumper cables, and a citizen's band (CB) radio seem like extras, but if you don't bring them, Murphy's Law says you'll regret it. A portable hand winch is definitely worth considering, and although your vehicle might not get stuck, someone else's could. On every trip, one gallon of water per person per day is the minimum. Several military MREs (Meals Ready to Eat), high-energy bars, or other similar, long shelf-life foods should always be kept in the vehicle in addition to what-ever trip goodies you tote along in the cooler. Rain gear, wool blankets, a heavy-duty flashlight, an emergency medical kit, a multipurpose tool, road flares, and a vehicle fire extinguisher are also valuable in an emergency situation. A GPS receiver can be a great tool, but don't forget the maps!

Photograph by Joel Klandrud

Photograph by Ray Bangs

Highway driving is worlds apart from the off-road experience. If you see a rock while cruising along the interstate, you avoid it, but sometimes, while off-roading, you need to drive right over that rock so you can keep going on the trail. Experience is the only way to learn how to be an off-road driver; however, it's much easier (and cheaper!) to enlist the support of others rather than trying to learn everything on your own. Off-road driving clinics, regularly taught by people who love to share their experience and knowledge, are a great option, but finding out about these classes can be difficult. If you do find one, they are often full. So one of the best and most accessible ways to learn more about four-wheeling is to join a club. All over Arizona, there are dozens of off-roading clubs for just about every make and model of vehicle as well as every experience level of driver.

The Arizona Xterra Club (AZXC) is based in Phoenix, but it has members from across the state and frequently welcomes out-of-state visitors. The AZXC is one of the most active off-roading clubs with monthly meetings as well as monthly Xcursions, off-

road weekend adventures that are perfectly suited for recreational SUVs. The one catch, of course, is that you can only join if you drive a Nissan Xterra! Luckily, numerous other clubs for other kinds of vehicles exist. One interesting club is the Arizona Virtual Jeep Club (AZVJC), which started and is still based in cyberspace. Hundreds of Jeepers from all over Arizona chat on the AZVJC message boards to plan weekend outings, discuss vehicle modifications, and exchange tips and ideas. As you get more involved with any of the clubs, you'll soon realize that off-roading encompasses everything from driving on an old forest road with your 2WD SUV to extreme rock-crawling with custom built, specially-modified trucks. Your level of participation is up to you, and as it is with all forms of recreation, the more you put into it, the more you'll get out of it.

Off-roading clubs are very strong supporters of Tread Lightly!, a nonprofit organization dedicated to the preservation of wild areas and the education of off-road drivers. In many of the clubs, education is the focal point where members learn how to minimize the environmental impact of their off-road activities. Another group, the Arizona State Association of 4-Wheel Drive Clubs (ASA4WDC), is heavily involved in organizing all the off-roading clubs in the state. The ASA4WDC volunteers thousands of hours each year to help rebuild areas destroyed by careless drivers, cleaning primitive camp sites, stringing

Photograph by Ray Bangs

fences, and working with wildlife habitat, all to promote responsible, off-highway recreation and to keep public land and trail closures to a minimum. The annual jamboree attracts hundreds of off-road enthusiasts and is another great way to meet more fun-loving folks.

One great advanced beginner route (requiring 4WD), just northeast of Phoenix, follows Forest Road 143 from Four Peaks to Roosevelt Lake. Plentiful camping options, miles of hiking paths, and a maze of additional off-roading trails can easily make this into a weekend. The spectacular scenery of the Four Peaks is well worth a day trip. The route takes approximately six hours, barring any mechanical difficulties. With the higher elevation, this is one of the few close-to-Phoenix areas that sees winter snow regularly, so a particularly heavy snowfall can even close the route. Erosion may create difficult sections in the road, so be sure to contact the Tonto Basin Ranger District before your trip. If you are planning on camping, ask about any updates on campsites.

As you explore the lesser-traveled routes of the Arizona backcountry, you'll begin to appreciate the wild land even more. You might even become an active participant in the off-roading community. Even if you only pack some camping gear and head out with the family or a few friends, getting off the paved road is a great weekend escape. And remember, tread lightly, have fun, and always be prepared.

Directions

From Mesa follow State Route 87 north to Forest Road 143 (Four Peaks Road) and turn right. Stay on FR 143 to SR 188. Turn left (north) on SR 188 and head back towards SR 87. When you get to SR 87, turn left (south) to return to the Valley.

Off-Roading Clubs

Arizona State Association of 4WD Clubs, www.asa4wdc.org
Arizona Virtual Jeep Club, www.azvjc.org
Arizona Xterra Club, www.azxterraclub.com

For More Information

Arizona State Parks, Off Highway Vehicle (OHV) Program, 866/463-6648, www.azohv.com
Tread Lightly, 800/966-9900, www.treadlightly.org

Recommended Reading

Hanson, Johnathan. *Backroad Adventuring in Your Sport Utility Vehicle.*
New York, NY: Ragged Mountain Press, 2000.
Massey, Peter. *Backcountry Adventures: Arizona.*
Castle Rock, CO: Swagman Publishing, 2001.

⑧ Peralta Canyon Trail #102

Hiking the Treasure of the Superstitions

Medium
$0–$500

Peralta Canyon Trail #102 is one of Arizona's most popular hikes, rich in local folklore and history, and some say rich in gold. At only an hour east of Phoenix, the popularity of this area located in the Superstition Mountains warranted recent upgrades of the facilities, including a restroom and an expanded parking lot. However, this improvement comes with a cost; a small fee is charged to park your vehicle for the day. As if you were parking your car in downtown Phoenix, an electronic parking meter greets you at the entrance. For those of you who forget to bring cash, credit cards are even accepted.

A park ranger is often posted at the trailhead, spinning yarns about the area and pointing hikers to their trails. Any big-city similarity ends, though, just a few steps down the path. Unprepared people often attempt this trail, but you will see them quickly turn back. With many rugged and rocky sections, the Peralta Canyon Trail offers excellent and interesting hiking year-round, but be ready with the proper gear, including good boots and a hydration pack full of cool water, especially if you choose to go in the heat of summer.

Photograph by Joel Klandrud

Luckily, several cool, shaded areas seem to be strategically located. Smaller children may find this hike too difficult, but generally this 4.5-mile trail is accessible for most. Allow three to four hours to complete the up and back loop. Begin your hike at the north side of the parking lot. Just past the trailhead is a junction where you want to take a left and enter the Superstition Wilderness Area. Going right leads you to Bluff Springs and the Lost Dutchman trails, including Red Tanks Divide.

Though it lacks some punch in comparison to the evocative trail names that surround it, Peralta makes up for it in historical richness. The canyon is named after Don Miguel Peralta, a Spaniard, who supposedly found gold in the Superstition Mountains. According to legend, fact, or campfire tale (depending on your view), the Peralta family made many trips to exploit the mine, but in 1848, the mining party was ambushed. A younger cousin named Carlos and his brother managed to escape back to Mexico. Years later, German fortune-seeker Jacob Waltz, known locally as the "Dutchman," rediscovered the mines. Another German, Jacob Weiser, joined Waltz to excavate the mine.

They soon found themselves partnered with the now older Carlos Peralta who had returned with a small group to mine the riches. Deciding there was enough gold for everybody, they teamed together to increase their chances of success. The threat of raids forced them to work at night and to be secretive when entering the area. Peralta carved stone maps leading to the entrance of the mine, but in 1874, on the trek back to Mexico, he was killed in an ambush. Waltz and Weiser looked about the area and tried to once again locate the mine, but the maps had disappeared.

More recently, in 1954, one of Peralta's maps was found by Travis Tumlinson, an Oregon police officer vacationing in Arizona. Over the years, Tumlinson found other maps that pointed the way to Peralta's mine, now better known as the Lost Dutchman Mine. However, even with these maps, the mines have never been found. One theory is that Peralta deceptively marked the maps to throw off anyone wanting to steal the gold, while others maintain that a curse was put over the land to forever close up the entrance.

Today, the State of Arizona has designated much of the area as the Lost Dutchman State Park, which prevents people from digging and blasting apart the land, but also presents a tricky situation if anyone does find the gold. Many treasure hunters do not mind the regulations, as they believe that the mines are actually not within the canyon. Still others, relying on the new "evidence" in the maps, maintain that the mines must be there and are just waiting to be found. Unfortunately for those following the tales of riches, the geological portrait of the Superstition Mountains, mostly volcanic rhyolite and tuff, is not typically gold-bearing. Nonetheless, the legend persists.

With all this history in mind, don't forget to stop and take a look at all the natural beauty that surrounds you. At the first rest stop, look back on your trail. You will see nothing but mountains stretching to the horizon. A small creek dribbles past several sections of the path, which provides just enough moisture for the sparse vegetation along the way. Make sure you take advantage of the shady areas, as the entire trail is uphill and rocky. Many photo opportunities also present themselves along the trail, especially with the unusually-shaped geology. Apache Rock looks like a dragon's head from one angle, but if you go a little farther away and wait for the sun to play its shadow games, and you'll see all kinds of shapes revealed.

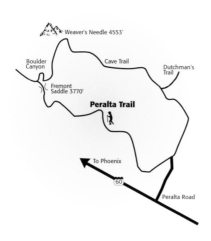

After just over two miles of a steady, but not too difficult ascent, you'll reach Fremont's Saddle. Named after John Fremont, the leader of many American survey expeditions, this saddle offers one of the best views in central Arizona. In the center of Boulder Canyon is Weaver's Needle, a 4,553-foot rock spire named for the 19th century mining woman Pauline Weaver. Be sure to bring plenty of film for this spectacular backdrop. For the more adventurous type, it is possible to venture deeper into the Superstition Wilderness, even right up to the base of Weaver's Needle. Many opt to pack a light tent and camp further into the area.

With plenty of trails in the area, many people decide to turn this one-day adventure into a

Photograph by Ray Bangs

weekend. Camping is conveniently located nearby at the Lost Dutchman State Park for a small fee per night. Those seeking more luxurious accommodations should retreat to the lush Gold Canyon Golf Resort, where activities such as golf or horseback riding can take up the rest of your weekend. With a range of $125 to $230 per night, it is a pricier way to experience the area, but it also provides the convenience and luxury of a five-star hotel.

Even if you don't find gold during your stay in Peralta Canyon, at less than an hour from Phoenix, it is a spectacular scenic escape, a hike that truly takes your breath away. So no matter how you decide to escape into Peralta Canyon, be sure not to stray too far from the trail...you just might stumble upon the mine.

Directions

Take US Hwy 60 east from Phoenix to Peralta Road, which is 14 miles past Apache Junction, just after milepost 204. Turn left (north) on Peralta Road (Forest Service Road 77) and drive approximately 7 miles to the parking lot at its end. Several trails begin from here.

Outfitters

Apache Trail Tours (see coupon pg 203), 480/982-7661, www.apachetrailtours.com
Gold Canyon Golf Resort (see coupon pg 203), 6100 S. Kings Ranch Road, Gold Canyon, AZ, 800/624-6445, www.gcgr.com

For More Information

U.S. Forest Service, Tonto National Forest, Phoenix, AZ, 602/225-5200, www.fs.fed.us/r3/tonto

Recommended Reading

Carlson, Jack. *Hikers Guide to the Superstition Wilderness: With History and Legends of Arizona's Lost Dutchman Gold Mine.* Tempe, AZ: Clear Creek Publishers, 1995.
Glover, Thomas. *The Lost Dutchman Mine of Jacob Waltz, Part 1: The Golden Dream.* Phoenix, AZ: Cowboy Miner Productions, 2000.
Glover, Thomas. *The Lost Dutchman Mine of Jacob Waltz, Part II: The Holmes Manuscript.* Phoenix, AZ: Cowboy Miner Productions, 2000.

9 Rent a Harley

Cruise the Southwest

Medium
$250–$500+

Highway 64—The Grand Canyon's East Rim Drive
Route 66—The Mother Road
Old Route 666—The Devil's Highway

If these names put images of pristine desert and curious history into your head, then scenic driving is something you should try. It's a good way to see the countryside without having to invest in a lot of gear (outside of the vehicle, that is) or take on difficult adventures that may be more work than leisure. Every year, thousands of tourists and locals pack up their families and take off on our desert highways, taking in sunsets and vistas, and consuming mass quantities of film in the process. However, these car-bound masses miss out on some things. There's no wind whipping their jackets; they don't smell the clean, city-free air with the AC running and the windows closed tight; and "cruising old 66 in the front seat of my trusty Volvo" just doesn't have as much romance to it.

When you think about it, there really is only one way to see Arizona's highways and byways—on the broad leather seat of a motorcycle. This state is steeped in bike lore. Peter Fonda and Dennis Hopper cruised through our state on their way to Louisiana in *Easy Rider*; Sonny Barger, the founder of the Hell's Angels in Oakland, CA, runs a motorcycle shop in Cave Creek near Phoenix; and Arizona is one of the few states to let riders decide whether or not to wear a helmet. All this, along with the year-round sunshine, makes Arizona a haven for riders of all skill levels.

Of course, the most popular American icon behind all this lore is the Harley Davidson. Founded in 1903 in Milwaukee, the company quickly grew during the first half of the century, and by 1953, Harley was the only American manufacturer of motorcycles. In the 1960s and 1970s, the Harley became the bike of choice for outlaw bikers like the Hell's Angels, but in recent decades a broader part of the American public is realizing that motorcycles aren't restricted to your stereotypical biker. As the annual Harley Davidson Motorcycle Fest in Sturgis, North Dakota clearly shows (over 550,000 enthusiasts showed up in 2000), Harleys, and motorcycles in general, are for everybody who wants to take the time and learn how to ride.

Now that you know your status on a Harley will be acceptable to the neighbors, go out and rent one for the weekend. Obviously, you'll need a motorcycle license before you rent a Harley, and some rental companies require a few years of riding experience as well. And even though Arizona doesn't require a helmet, you should seriously consider wearing one.

Courtesy of Harley-Davidson

There are some Arizona natives who, because of the heat and the lack of a helmet law, ride around town in shorts and flip-flops. Don't be that person, mostly because it's a good way to lose all the skin on your legs pretty easily. Prepare for the ride and you will maximize your enjoyment.

If you didn't bring your leathers, you'll be fine. Most rental companies provide clothing to rent as well as free helmets for use with their bikes. Prices are determined by two things: the type of Harley and the amount of time you want to rent the bike for. If you want to rent an Anniversary Edition Heritage Springer, it'll cost quite a bit more than if you want to go with the base Sportster. You can take off for an afternoon or go on the statewide tour, meandering around for days on the highways and byways. In a weekend, you will get a lengthy tour in even if you take your time, and most rental companies will be glad to help you create an itinerary guaranteed to let you do the most with your time.

This being said, everyone who rides should partake in this amazing way to see our countryside. In the Southwest alone there are as many good runs to make as there are highways. But one in particular brings together all the most amazing qualities of a good motorcycle ride—Monument Valley Tribal Park. Though the park entrance is just over the Utah state line, most of the park is in Arizona, and it is some of the most breathtaking land in the state. You'll recognize the desert around you from hundreds of Hollywood westerns. This area is a popular place for shooting the southwestern landscape, and you can't help but know why as you ride past Sunset Crater National Monument, Navajo National Monument, and many of the other famous points of interest. Being out in the open, free on a Harley to feel everything going on around you, can only bring all of this grandeur closer to you.

Whether you are a native Arizonan or just visiting, you should also look into what motorcycle runs are going on during the time you'll have your Harley. Since Arizona is so bike-friendly, there is a large and supportive motorcycle community here, complete with

Courtesy of Arizona Office of Tourism

a ton of resources. If you visit the Arizona Confederation of Motorcycle Clubs website and click on the calendar, you'll find events of all kinds to attend. Each entry provides a "for more information" number, so just call for details.

One event that always draws a large crowd is Arizona Bike Week. It is held in the spring, and it is one of the largest motorcycle gatherings in the country. There are races at Firebird Raceway, runs all over the state, parties galore, and generally a good time to be had by all. It's a good time to be in town if you love motorcycles. Just ask your rental company when the next Bike Week is, as they're sure to know.

Like hang gliding or mountaineering, this is not an adventure for everyone, as it does take a little time to learn how to ride and earn the motorcycle endorsement on your driver's license. But if you are a rider, Arizona is a must-see destination, and if you don't ride yet, maybe now is a good time to start. After all, what better way to see the stomping grounds of the cowboys than on the back of an iron horse.

Directions

To get to Monument Valley Tribal Park from Flagstaff take Hwy 89 north for 68 miles. Turn east onto Hwy 160 and drive 90 miles to Kayenta. Look for the Hwy 163 signs pointing towards Monument Valley, another 25 miles away.

Outfitters

Billy Ray's Hogg Heaven (see coupon pg 203), Lake Havasu City, AZ
877/464-7933, www.hoggheavenrentals.com
Sedona Rent-A-Hawg at the Hemp & Hawg (see coupon pg 203), Sedona, AZ
877/736-8242, www.sedonaharleyrentals.com
Western States Motorcycle Rentals and Tours (see coupon pg 203), Phoenix, AZ
602/943-9030, www.azmcrent.com

For More Information

Arizona Confederation of Motorcycle Clubs, www.azcmc.com
Harley Davidson Motorcycles, www.harley-davidson.com

Recommended Reading

Barger, Ralph "Sonny." *Hell's Angel: The Life and Times of Sonny Barger and the Hell's Angels Motorcycle Club.* New York, NY: William Morrow & Co, 2000.
Berke, Martin C. *Motorcycle Journeys Through the Southwest: You Don't Have to Get Lost to Find the Good Roads.* North Conway, NH: Whitehorse Press, 1994.
Del Monte, Frank. *Motorcycle Arizona.* Phoenix, AZ: Golden West Publications, 1994.

Bicycle Tour

Get Your Kicks Pedaling Route 66

The ultimate active vacation is bicycle touring. You don't have to be an expert cyclist, you don't have to be in great shape, and you don't need to spend a fortune on gear. Bike touring is addictive, too. It's such incredible recreation that once most people take a shorter tour, they're hooked. It starts with just a day trip or a weekend escape, but then quickly turns into a passion. Pedaling across the United States is the extreme culmination of this delight, but even the fastest riders take a month to complete that journey. The best way to start this experience is to try two or three days on the road, and then once you're hooked, start saving up the vacation time for your next tour.

Historic Route 66 is well known as one of the first great east-to-west American highways, connecting the charming small towns between Chicago and Los Angeles. The famous road, although now only a shadow of its former self, still embodies that American passion for exploring. Tens of thousands of people drive the highway each year, but a smaller group of pedal enthusiasts have found that bicycling is a great way to relive part of its legendary history.

While much of the original route has been lost to time since its completion in 1938, Arizona proudly claims one stretch of this historic road where the lore and love of the open highway have not completely disappeared. For a great weekend getaway, try pedaling along Route 66 from Seligman to Topock. This 158-mile stretch of pavement is the longest intact and uninterrupted section of the "Mother Road" remaining in the U.S., and it still maintains much of the original character and feel of the early 1900s mining towns, proving that rural America is not yet completely lost to technology.

Photograph by Ray Bangs

In its prime, traveling Route 66 was an adventure, leading people through the American frontier where the pioneering spirit was very much alive. During the Great Depression, unemployed workers migrated west searching for a better job and a better life. However, in the 1940s with American involvement in World War II leading to gasoline rationing and a significant slowing in vehicle production, few people traveled at all, let alone along Route 66. Then, as the GIs started coming home, the baby boom erupted and families really started to drive. The Depression and the War were finally over so it was time to throw the kids in

Courtesy of Arizona Office of Tourism

the car and visit all the places only seen before on postcards. In the late 1940s and through most of the 50s, people sought the journey much more than just the destination. All along Route 66, travelers found small towns that still featured windshield-cleaning gas station attendants, drive-up (not drive-through) fast food stops, and motels where guests actually talked to each other. Route 66 was the ultimate road trip.

In 1957, President Eisenhower, after seeing how smoothly the German Autobahn system operated, championed the National Interstate Highway System. With these plans, Route 66 saw its eventual demise. The new mega-highways bypassed many small towns, and only the towns closest to the interstates, like Seligman, were able to hold on. With the official opening of Interstate 40 in October of 1984, Williams garnered the distinction of being the last Route 66 town bypassed by the Interstate. Shortly afterwards, the familiar highway signs of Route 66 were taken down.

Today, Route 66 is still rockin' with the growing interest in American nostalgia. Classic cars and Harley Davidson motorcycles rumble along the route every day, especially in the summers when classic auto "fun runs" and motorcycle "rallies" take these cities by storm. The first weekend of May signifies the "Annual Route 66 Fun Run," sponsored and organized by the Historic Route 66 Association of Arizona. Since 1988, this event has attracted people from all over the world. With the parade of classic cars starting in Seligman, this 140-mile event is the perfect opportunity to get on your bike. The road certainly won't be lonely!

The towns you will pass through each offer their individual charm to the celebration, ranging from their historical buildings and souvenir shops to Native American dances and BBQs. All in all, there are plenty of opportunities for exercise and fun! If you stay in Seligman or any other towns along the route for the event, be sure to make hotel or campground reservations well in advance. Although there is no designated bike lane, there is enough room for bicyclists. Additionally, this stretch of Route 66 is suitable for bike touring all year long, but remember to bring warmer clothes and raingear; even in the warmer months, the temperatures can drop unexpectedly. To haul your gear, visit your local bike store and invest in a set of panniers—bags that fit on the rear rack—as they are more comfortable than a backpack and will comfortably hold all your extra gear.

Without the comfort and protection of a car, you need to be prepared in case you are forced to brave the elements as well.

The first sign of civilization west of Seligman is 25 miles away at the Grand Canyon Caverns, one of the largest dry caves in the United States. Guided 45-minute walking tours are offered every half hour and begin with a 21-story elevator descent. Services include a restaurant, motel, gift shop, and campground. Continuing on, you will enter the southern tip of the Hualapai Indian Reservation, and after 12 miles, you'll reach their headquarters in the town of Peach Springs. Food and lodging is available. Another eight miles of pedaling will take you to Truxton, a small community serving as a reminder of the once prosperous life along the "Main Street of America." If you are taking three days to pedal the 140 miles from Seligman to Topock, no other hotels are available until Kingman, which is another 40 miles.

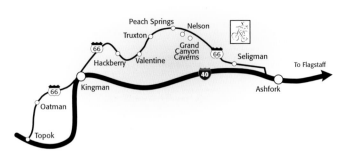

As you spend the next two days pedaling along, passing through Valentine, Hackberry, Kingman, and Oatman before finally reaching Topock, you'll see how this newly rekindled interest in the "Mother Road" has helped preserve these Route 66 towns, as well as the road itself. Americans are nostalgic for the good ol' days, the times when life didn't blaze along on expressways at 90 miles per hour, the days of past when travelers on Route 66 kept their speed around 45. Pedaling is one of the best ways to really slow down, forget about climate control, let your hair blow in the breeze, and focus again on the journey. At least you can still have a leather seat!

Directions

Seligman is 75 miles west of Flagstaff, just north of I-40. The bike route follows Historic Route 66 west to Topock.

For More Information

GABA, Greater Arizona Bicycle Association, www.sportsfun.com/gaba
Historic Route 66 Association of Arizona, The Powerhouse Visitor Center
120 W. Andy Devine Ave. (Route 66), Kingman, AZ , 928/753-5001,
www.azrt66.com

Recommended Reading

Coello, Dennis. *Bicycle Touring in Arizona.* Flagstaff, AZ: Northland Publishing, 1988.
Langley, Jim. *Bicycling Magazine's Complete Guide to Bicycle Maintenance and Repair.*
    Emmaus, PA: Rodale Press, 1999.
Lovett, Richard. *The Essential Touring Cyclist: A Complete Guide for the Bicycle Traveler.*
    New York, NY: Ragged Mountain Press, 2000.
Snyder, Tom. *Route 66: Traveler's Guide and Roadside Companion.*
    New York, NY: St. Martin's Press, 2000.

Skydiving
Surfing the Desert Sky

There's definitely something wrong about jumping out of a perfectly good airplane. Every year, however, thousands of people do it, and many who jump once keep on jumping. So what's the attraction? Are skydivers people trying to fly like a bird or is it just the adrenaline rush? It's hard to say. But after George Bush Sr. took flight, more and more people are considering it at any age.

Year round jumping, made possible by our mild weather, makes Arizona one of the world's most popular drop zones. A global community has developed around skydiving and huge annual events, known as "boogies," are a hit with both participants and spectators. Of course, the views are better from above! So if seeing the world from 13,000 feet interests you, take that first step out an open door, and take that first plunge towards a fast-approaching earth.

To maintain safety while skydiving (no that's not an oxymoron), regulations and training have been established, and the modern equipment in mechanical terms is nearly fail-safe. A first jump is almost always a "tandem," where you and your instructor are attached together to the same parachute. Since you are in front with your own altimeter and ripcord, the sensation is very similar to flying solo. Skydive Arizona takes first-time jumpers to 13,000 feet, so you'll be able to enjoy almost a full minute of free fall. Stop reading right now and watch the clock for sixty seconds.

Yes, that's a long time!

After that full minute of adrenaline and excitement, you pull the ripcord. The canopy deploys and the instructor shows you how to steer and fly the parachute safely towards the landing zone. The most dangerous part of skydiving, however, is the landing, so do exactly what your experienced instructor says; he or she wants to walk away from the jump just as much as you do.

Skydive Arizona is one of the most popular jump schools in the Grand Canyon State and is the world's largest skydiving resort. That tandem jump you just finished is the primer to the Accelerated Skydiving Program, where you can become a certified jumper.

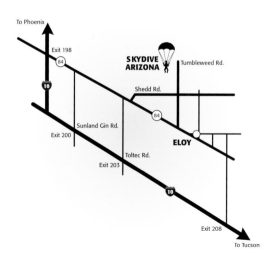

After that initial jump, you can decide if skydiving is something you want to become more seriously involved in. The first tandem jump costs $145 and it usually takes less than four hours. Or, you can pay an additional $135 for a second jump and make a whole day out of it.

If you decide to make a weekend out of this adventure, you can spend the second day doing another tandem jump or preparing for your first Accelerated Freefall (AFF), also from 13,000 feet. If you choose the latter, a six to eight hour ground school prepares you for this first AFF jump, where you'll be wearing your own chute system and will be accompanied

Photograph by Brent Finley

by two jumpmasters. You'll experience another minute of freefall, and then pull your ripcord and fly the parachute. An instructor communicating via radio will guide you through the landing. The AFF program involves eight instructional levels and is the quickest route to becoming a licensed skydiver. If you have already tried skydiving, this basic course of eight to twelve jumps (several may need to be repeated), can be completed in a three-day weekend.

Skydiving can quickly become a lifestyle. The United States Parachute Association (USPA) administers a system of proficiency ratings, and an "A license," being the first level, requires 20 to 30 jumps and usually takes 10 to 14 days. This license costs $245 and is easily attainable over several weekends. With an A license and your own gear, you can jump almost anywhere.

The Skydive Arizona drop zone features a full-service bar and restaurant, swimming pool, pro shop, and very inexpensive bunkhouse accommodations. The bunkhouse is basic yet comfortable; however, visitors must supply their own pillows, blankets, and sheets. The cost is a very reasonable $5 per night and is even free during June, July, and August. A kitchen area, sinks, toilets, showers, and coin-operated laundry machines are conveniently located for visitor use. Reservations for the bunkhouse are not accepted unless you are taking an A-License student package.

If you want to go even cheaper, students can camp free for a day or two, and longer term camping costs only a buck a day. Another option, just a short distance away, is the new RV park with 40 hookups, and there are an additional eight slots located right next to the drop zone. The cost is $12 to $15 per day plus tax. Advance reservations are highly recommended, especially for the busier winter months.

Interestingly, most skydivers are in great shape. Jumping not only helps build confidence in your life, but it's somewhat physically demanding as well. Skydive Arizona even

41

Photograph by Brent Finley

offers an onsite fitness center complete with free weights, Nautilus machines, and more. Be forewarned though—you cannot go to Skydive Arizona expecting to get in shape. They have a strict weight limit of 220 pounds, as the chutes are certified to that limit. And even though it is possible for a person weighing 240 pounds to use the same rig, if you're even a single pound over the maximum, you can't jump! Skydive Arizona's excellent safety record is so perfect because they do not take any unnecessary risks. Additionally, the minimum age is 18, again with no exceptions.

Skydiving is easy! The only tough part is working up the courage to step out of that perfectly good airplane. Basic human nature simply goes against falling, especially falls that could potentially be dangerous or even fatal. However, many people (including the authors) who have been terrified of heights all their lives, have found that skydiving promotes an entirely new perspective on taking risks…and the risks in skydiving are actually quite minimal. But if you're still concerned, take heed to this fact: skydiving is actually safer than driving your car! And, of course, jumping from 13,000 feet and falling 120 miles per hour is a lot more exciting than driving. Most even call it fun.

Directions

From Phoenix follow eastbound I-10 towards Tucson to exit 198. Turn left onto Hwy 84, go seven miles, and go left on Tumbleweed Road (look for the airport sign). Drive two miles, and the skydiving school is on the left of the large grassy area.

Outfitters

Skydive Arizona (see coupon pg 205), 4900 N. Taylor Rd., Eloy, AZ
    800/759-3483 (within Arizona), 800/858-5867, www.skydiveaz.com

For More Information

Groundrush Skydiving Exhibition Team, Brent Finley Skydiving Cinematography
    www.brentfinley.com
United States Parachute Association, 703/836-3495, www.uspa.org

Recommended Reading

Turoff, Mike & Poynter, Dan. *Parachuting: The Skydiver's Handbook.*
    Santa Barbara, CA: Para Publishing, 1999.

Hiking the Grand Canyon

Bright Angel Trail and Hidden Havasupai

Difficult
$0–$500⁺

The Bright Angel Trail is one of the most popular hikes in the United States. You start at the South Rim of the Grand Canyon, and over the nine-mile trek you descend nearly a vertical mile before finally reaching the Colorado River. The Bright Angel Trail is fun and challenging (especially on the way up), so if you love hiking in Arizona, it should definitely be on your list. According to Stacy Pearson from the Arizona Office of Tourism, of the approximate five million Grand Canyon visitors each year, less than 200,000 step even one foot below the rim. Hiking the Bright Angel Trail is the perfect way to become part of this adventurous minority.

The first step to hiking Bright Angel is to secure the necessary backcountry permit from the Grand Canyon National Park Backcountry Office. The official Grand Canyon policy states that a "backcountry permit is required for overnight use of the backcountry, including overnight hiking, overnight horseback riding, overnight cross-country ski trips, off-river overnight hikes by river trip members, and overnight camping at rim sites other than developed campgrounds." You can apply up to four months in advance, and the earlier the better because the permit system is on a first-come, first-served basis. If you are feeling adventurous (and lucky), you can just show up at the park without advance permits and put your name on the waiting list for cancellations. If you think you will need a little more luxury than a tent, Phantom Ranch offers cabins and dorm-style rooms. Do not count on last-minute openings, though; often to get a space, you need to send in your applications months in advance.

Courtesy of Arizona Office of Tourism

While your permit application is in the works, start getting in shape. Just walking a half-hour every day won't hurt, but it certainly will not prepare you for ten hours of carrying a thirty-plus pound pack for ten miles with over a vertical mile drop in elevation. The best way to get in shape for hiking is by hiking. There are very few places in this world where you can't find a hilly area to hike, and even if the hills are small, that just means going up and down several times. Stair-climbing machines at the gym are boring, but they are a quick substitute for busier days. And a good thing to remember when you are getting in shape is that canyon hiking is the opposite of mountain climbing. This means you face the steep uphill climbs at the end of the hike when you are already tired; therefore, endurance is essential.

The next step to preparing for a Canyon hike, which can be quite a financial commitment, is to gather the necessary gear. You have the luxury of time, so don't be impulsive on your purchases. Outdoor recreation equipment

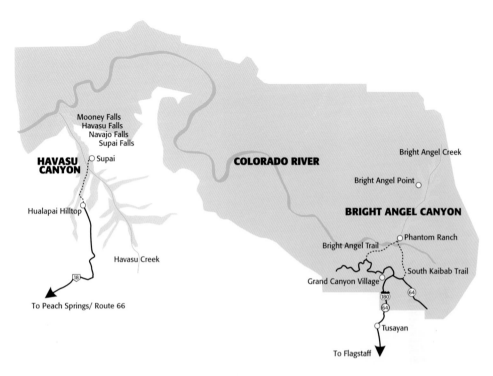

Mooney Falls
Havasu Falls
Navajo Falls
Supai Falls

HAVASU CANYON

○ Supai

Bright Angel Creek

COLORADO RIVER

Bright Angel Point ○

Hualapai Hilltop

BRIGHT ANGEL CANYON

Havasu Creek

Bright Angel Trail ·····○ Phantom Ranch

Grand Canyon Village ○

South Kaibab Trail

18

To Peach Springs/ Route 66

180
64

64

○ Tusayan

To Flagstaff

can be expensive, but it is important as hiking can be really tough on your knees, back, and feet, especially if you have ill-fitting equipment. Search the internet for good deals, take some time to research which features are desirable and which are just hype, and finally, find the best price. If you feel there is a good chance that this healthy, outdoor lifestyle will become more of an influence in your life, consider spending a little more money to buy better equipment. Of course, the fact remains that the people who inhabited the Grand Canyon over the past thousands of years never knew Gore-tex jackets, goose down sleeping bags, or graphite trekking poles. That is not to say that there weren't times when they wished they were a little warmer, a little cozier, or a little more sure-footed!

More than any other part of your body, your feet will be taking a serious pounding, so perfect-fitting hiking boots are essential. When you go to buy boots, make sure it's at the end of the day and ideally, after a long jog. This is the best way to make sure your feet are fully expanded just as they would be hiking. The old adage about gradually breaking in your boots is just that—old. Find boots that fit comfortably in the store, and then with use, they will become even more comfortable. If possible, take a few days and wear the boots around before your hike, as this will make them even more soft and comfortable.

The main corridor trails are the easiest and safest, with emergency phones located along the route. The Bright Angel Trail as well as the North and South Kaibab Trails are popular with first-time Canyon hikers. They are considered easy, but of course, that is relative to the Grand Canyon. The Park Rangers commonly tell a joke about how there are only two options of getting to the Colorado River—the hard way, and the harder way. With more Canyon hiking experience, try the Thunder River, South Bass, New Hance, and Tanner trails. The Boucher, North Bass, and Nankoweap trails are generally considered to be the most challenging of the major routes. For any of these trails, there are dozens of companies that offer everything from basic guided hikes to the fully outfitted, just-show-up luxury trips; prices vary greatly depending on services requested. Some of

Photograph by Ray Bangs

the best outfitters include Inner Gorge Trail Guides, Four Seasons Outfitters, Sky Island Treks, Canyon Rim Adventures, and Discovery Treks.

Although relatively few people tackle any of the Grand Canyon trails, if you really want to get away from the crowds, a very interesting option is to go west, where you'll still be in the Grand Canyon, but not technically in the National Park. Havasu Canyon is one of over 600 side canyons in the Grand Canyon, and to many, Arizona's most pristine paradise. It is located less than 35 miles from the South Rim Village as the crow flies, but with it's remoteness, is a 180-mile drive.

Hiking through Havasu Canyon to reach Supai, the most remote village in the U.S., is a somewhat rugged, but manageable eight-mile trek, plus an additional two miles to the camp-ground. From the Hualapai Hilltop trailhead, you start down a series of switchbacks, which drastically drop in elevation, but are only difficult on the way back out. After the first mile, the trail flattens out considerably and becomes a scenic, downhill walk for the rest of the way. Although this trip can be self-organized, the far better option is to go with the experienced guides of Arizona Outback Adventures. They are definitely the experts and know all the hidden secrets; their guides spend an average of four days per week in Havasu Canyon!

Their "Ultimate Hike" trip departs in the afternoon and is followed by three full days of breathtaking adventure. The price includes everything from the first night's lodging at the Grand Canyon Caverns Inn to all the required permits and some of the best back-country food you will ever eat. This really can be the trip of your lifetime. If you have an extra day, the "Ultimate Hike Plus" is even better. The water of the refreshing travertine pools and waterfalls is the bluest blue you will ever see, and unlike other parts of the Grand Canyon, which can be quite desolate and barren, Havasu Canyon is a lush jungle of green due to its mineral rich waters.

Whether you try the self-planned trip down the Bright Angel Trail or the other, more advanced options such as exploring Havasu Canyon with an outfitter, hiking any part of the Grand Canyon is a difficult, yet spectacular accomplishment. Sadly, people get hurt and even die every year, so be prepared and be careful. Going below the rim is truly an adventure and always a wonderful journey. It's a shame that many people living in Arizona visit the rim once and then take the Grand Canyon for granted. It is somehow easy to forget how grand it really is. Go back, hike to the bottom, and you will find yourself humble once again.

Directions

To get to the Grand Canyon from Phoenix follow I-17 north to Flagstaff. Take US-180 north to AZ Route 64 N to the south entrance. For Havasu Canyon, follow I-17 north towards Flagstaff. After 60 miles, at exit 262, merge onto AZ-69 towards Prescott. Drive 34 miles and turn north on US-89 towards Ash Fork. After 45 miles, turn west on I-40 to Seligman. From Seligman, take Historic Route 66 west towards Peach Springs. Just past the Grand Canyon Caverns Inn, take Route 18 north for approximately 60 miles to the trailhead at Hualapai Hilltop. Seligman offers the last gasoline services available on this route.

Outfitters

Havasu Canyon Outfitters, Arizona Outback Adventures (see coupon pg 205)
    480/945-2881, www.azoutbackadventures.com
Grand Canyon Outfitters, Canyon Dreams (see coupon pg 205)
    888/731-4680, www.canyondreams.com
Canyon Rim Adventures (see coupon pg 205), 800/897-9633
    www.canyonrimadventures.com
Discovery Treks (see coupon pg 205), 888/256-8731, www.discoverytreks.com
Four Seasons Outfitters (see coupon pg 205), 877/272-5032, www.fsoutfitters.com
Grand Canyon Hikes (see coupon pg 205), 877/506-6233, www.grandcanyonhikes.com
High Sonoran Adventures (see coupon pg 205), 480/614-3331, www.highsonoran.com
Inner Gorge Trail Guides (see coupon pg 207), 877/787-4453, www.innergorge.com
Sky Island Treks (see coupon pg 207), 877/944-5348, www.skyislandtreks.com

For More Information

Grand Canyon National Park Backcountry Office, Permit Information,
    www.nps.gov/grca, 928/638-7875
    (Park Rangers do not take permit requests over the phone.)
Havasupai Tourist Enterprises, Tourist Office: 928/448-2141, Lodging: 928/448-2111
Phantom Ranch, AmFac Parks & Resorts, 303/297-2757, www.amfac.com
Recorded Grand Canyon Trail Conditions & Information, 928/638-7888 (24 hr)

Recommended Reading

Butchart, Harvey. *Grand Canyon Treks: 12,000 Miles Through the Grand Canyon.*
    Bishop, CA: Spotted Dog Press, 1988.
Iliff, Flora. *People of the Blue Water: A Record of Life among the Walapai and Havasupai Indians.* Tucson, AZ: University of Arizona Press, 1985.
Thybony, Scott. *Official Guide to Hiking the Grand Canyon.*
    Grand Canyon, AZ: Grand Canyon Association, 1997.
Whitney, Stephen. *A Field Guide to the Grand Canyon.*
    Seattle, WA: The Mountaineers, 1996.

Photograph by Peter Zwagerman

Kayaking the Salt River
Rock and Roll Whitewater

As warmer weather starts to melt the snow of the White Mountains, the waters of the White and Black Rivers splash together with the Cibecue, Carrizo, Canyon, and Cherry Creek tributaries, all of which flow into the Salt River to create a watery playground for whitewater kayakers. The Upper Salt River, located two hours east of Phoenix, is a paddler's paradise. In the spring, the chilly whitewater of the Salt River is raging. For Arizona kayakers, it's time to rock and roll—you better avoid the rocks and you better have a good Eskimo roll!

While dams regulate the flows of most other rivers, the Upper Salt is left untamed. Since nothing but nature controls the water flow, the winter snowpack in the White Mountains determines just how exciting the boating will be. Water levels fluctuate daily. March and April mark the peak of the season, but dramatic differences can occur with changes in weather. Even a warm day or two at higher elevations can melt enough snow to turn a lazy flow of 1000 cubic feet per second (cfs) into torrents of 12,000 cfs or more. Heavy rains can have the same effect, but Arizona weather is always unpredictable. A late snowstorm and below-freezing temperatures might greet you the next day. The best insurance is to hope for the best but be prepared for anything. Check out the Forest Service website for up-to-the-minute water flows.

Even after you have acquired the necessary gear, learning to kayak is not a one-day course. It can take months and even years to become proficient enough to tackle the more difficult rapids, so it's much better and safer to gradually build your skills. Rapids are rated on a scale from I-VI. Beginner level Class I rapids consist of fast moving water with easy to negotiate hazards and only a low risk of injury if you are forced to exit from the boat. The highest level rapid is the extreme Class VI, which is considered unrunnable by most sane people. Groups of expert paddlers might occasionally attempt Class VI rapids when water levels are favorable, but only after serious scouting and taking all safety precautions. The risks grow more significant as the ratings get higher, so don't plan on buying a kayak in early March and then spending the following weekend on the Upper Salt. With its rapids rated from Class III to Class IV+, (advanced intermediates and experts only), not knowing what you are doing might kill you.

In order to become proficient enough to survive the Class III and IV rapids, you must first learn the fundamentals and different techniques of kayaking, and then reinforce these skills with continuous practice. The logical first step is to take lessons from an expert; Permagrin Canoe and Kayak School in Tempe is the perfect place to start. They have an excellent selection of whitewater boats to rent or purchase, and there is even a pool on-site to try them out. Owner Peter Zwagermen will make sure you are fitted properly in a kayak that suits the type of water you want to paddle.

Their beginner weekend courses are taught in the pool where you learn the basics like wet-exits, stroke techniques, and rescues. Advanced beginner classes build on your previous knowledge and then start to examine topics like river current, flow, rapid classification, and other safety issues. Practice is continually emphasized and soon you'll be confidently ready to try the slower moving currents on the Lower Salt, Gila, and Verde Rivers.

In the winter months, the water on these local rivers can be quite low and slow, not to mention icy cold. Wetsuits are definitely required. As a much warmer and wetter

Photograph by Peter Zwagerman

alternative, the Permagrin School has also helped create one of the best indoor whitewater programs in the country. The large wave pool at the Tempe Kiwanis Recreation Center is open from October through February to help kayakers keep their paddles sharp with that promise of spring whitewater not far off. The machine-created waves are very similar to coastal breakers and can be set to 10 different wave patterns. Four-foot swells pack plenty of power, so your kayaking moves are limited only by your imagination and skill. With 85° F air and water temperatures, artificial surf is the way to go in the winter.

After significant time in your boat and a healthy boost of courage, the Upper Salt will be calling your name. Be prepared for a very scenic escape! The Salt River Canyon is known in many circles as the mini-Grand with its rugged geology and picturesque vistas. Day trips and weekend camping trips in this winding canyon are both possible. First-timers are highly encouraged to go with other experienced

kayakers to ensure a safer trip. A good way to find these experienced boaters is to get involved with a club like the Desert Paddlers or the Central Arizona Paddlers, both fun-loving groups that will warmly welcome you into the kayaking community. Besides offering advice, helping you learn a few new tricks, and finding others to go kayaking with, these clubs also participate in a number of community service events.

Getting onto the Upper Salt requires a $15 per person per day permit from the White Mountain Apache tribe. Camping fees may also be required. If you wish to paddle past Gleason Flats into the Salt River Wilderness for an extended trip from March 1 to June 1, you must apply for a permit through the U.S. Forest Service lottery system. The limited application window runs from December 1 to January 31 each winter. As this stretch of river has grown more popular, restrictions on the number of private trips have been established and the Forest Service is considering cutting that number even lower. Always be sure to pack out your trash and leave no trace.

The takeout point for day-trippers is Cibecue Creek, located seven miles downstream of US-60. There's an excellent campground with an all-access road so for two-day trips, paddlers can stop here or continue farther downstream and camp along the river. The poorly maintained roads leading to the takeout at Gleason Flats are much more rugged and usually require 4WD. Remember that you must shuttle a vehicle to your takeout point before putting in or you'll have a long hike back!

Kayaking the Upper Salt is an incredible whitewater adventure for desert dwellers. While most tourists are out looking at the wildflowers in the spring, with a little practice and preparation over the winter, you'll be rockin' and rollin' through one of Arizona's most scenic and wild canyons in no time.

Directions

To get to the put in from Phoenix follow US-60 east to the Salt River Canyon Bridge approximately 40 miles north of Globe.

Outfitters

Canyons & Coastlines Kayak School, 602/258-6318, www.canyonsandcoastlines.com
Permagrin Kayak and Canoe School (see coupon pg 207), 107 E. Broadway Rd., Suite B
   Tempe, AZ, 480/755-1924, www.go-permagrin.com
Paddling Clubs, Central AZ Paddlers, 602/695-1407, www.azpaddlers.com
Desert Paddlers, 480/755-1924

For More Information

Kiwanis Recreation Center, 480/350-5201
Tempe Parks and Recreation, 480/350-5200
U.S. Forest Service, Tonto National Forest, Mesa Ranger District, 480/610-3300
White Mountain Apache Tribe (Permit Information), 928/338-4385

Recommended Reading

Hutchinson, Derek. *Eskimo Rolling.* Guilford, CT: Globe Pequot Press, 1999.
Nealy, William. *Kayak: The Animated Manual of Intermediate and Advanced
   Whitewater Technique.* Birmingham, AL: Menasha Ridge Press, 1988.
Stuhaug, Dennis. *Kayaking Made Easy: A Manual for Beginners with Tips for
   the Experienced.* Guilford, CT: Globe Pequot Press, 1998.

Summer

14 Salt River Tubing
A Floating Picnic

Easy
$0–$100

The temperatures are blazing, again, and it's 110° F in the shade. You wonder, "Is this furnace ever going to end? My legs are sticking to the car seats! Will it ever be cool again? I think I'm melting!"

The summer sun in central Arizona can definitely be frustrating and overpowering. You just want to escape the heat, the sweat, and the burning brightness that come with each new day. Our best advice is to get into your car, turn on the AC, drive about a half hour northeast of Phoenix, and cool off at the Salt River Recreation Area, the home of Salt River Tubing. This is a perfect way to enjoy the four months of hot, sometimes unbearable weather.

Tubing season usually lasts from mid-April to mid-September, seven days a week, weather and water flow permitting. The river can be surprisingly cold, so the best time to tube is when the thermometer is on the verge of exploding. With the Phoenix summers, that means quite a few great tubing days! And, as more people find out about it, the more people try it out. Thousands of tubers celebrate Memorial Day, Independence Day, and Labor Day holidays with a floating picnic on the river.

Salt River Tubing has been providing tube rentals and shuttle bus service since 1981 on the Lower Salt River in the Tonto National Forest. All you have to do is drive to the parking lot, grab your cooler, and go to the rental station. The cost of a tube rental and shuttle bus ride is approximately $10, but don't forget to rent a tube for the cooler. As tubing is a one-shot deal, you'll need to decide between trips lasting anywhere from one

Courtesy of Mesa Convention and Visitors Bureau

Photograph by Chris Tafoya

to five hours. Be aware that these times do fluctuate greatly with the water flows and your style of tubing. The busses will drop you off and pick you up after you are finished at a number of different points, so make sure you and your group are perfectly clear on where you will be picked up.

Great tubing is an art form. There are people who just go tubing, have fun, and enjoy it, but a few have figured out how to maximize the experience. A few simple rules, or tips, will get you well on your way to becoming a Zen master of tubing.

Rule #1: Never paddle. While some people are swimming and racing all over the river in their tubes, that just means serious chafing on their arms and legs. Let the river take you wherever it wants to. The scenery is spectacular in every direction. Some people bring sheets or large towels to put over their tube since they do get hot in the sun. This works, but so does splashing water on the tube occasionally. Of course, you may have to paddle once in a great while. Remember that the water here on the Lower Salt is shallow and filled with rocks so keep your butt up!

Rule #2: Tie your tube to the cooler tube. Not only is this a comfortable footrest, but it is also convenient; an ice-cold beer (or soda) tastes great on the river. You want to have easy access. Remember that no glass is allowed and only bring a hard plastic cooler. Styrofoam will be destroyed and is impossible to clean up. Don't forget to pack along at least 1 liter of water per person and "pre-hydrate" by drinking plenty of water before your tubing trip.

Rule #3: Slop on the sunscreen. Skin cancer is deadly and there's no reason to increase your chances by being careless. Regularly apply a fresh coat to help prevent a burn. The rays reflecting off the water intensify the sun's effects; you'll see foolish people glowing red when you get back to the parking lot. If you want to get a tan, don't worry…even with SPF 40 applied frequently, you'll still get some color and it will last longer. A hat is also a great idea.

Rule #4: Who says a hip-pack isn't cool! If you still have a hip-pack, the Salt River is the place to bring it. Strap it around your tube so the pouch is on the top. This nifty carrying case is the perfect storage spot for a camera, sunscreen, lip-balm, your car key, food, or anything else you want to keep dry. If your hip-pack is not waterproof, Ziploc bags inside the pack work well. Other items not to forget are old tennis shoes or sturdy sandals, sunglasses, a hat, a shirt, and rope to tether you to the cooler. Everything can (and usually does) get soaked on a tubing trip, but being prepared helps. Make sure you only bring your one car key and have some type of backup plan too. Every year, SCUBA divers cleaning up the river find hundreds of key chains, as well as sunglasses, watches, and wallets.

Rule #5: Clean up your trash and leave no trace! Tubing on the Salt River is a great experience, but unfortunately, you will see a lot of trash littering the shores for the length of your trip. Drink your beer and pack out your cans; just crush them up and put them back in the cooler. It's too simple! If a can gets away from you, retrieve it. And while you're at it, pick up the four cans you find along the way as well. If everyone does this, the river will start to look healthy again. Remember, tubing does not ruin the river, but tubers throwing trash everywhere does.

Rule #6: Do not participate in or encourage cliff jumping. Cliff jumping is very dangerous at the Salt River Recreation Area. People die every year, yet more continue to do it. Don't cheer them on and don't let any of your friends go. It may look like fun from a distance, and those doing it may not get hurt this time, but then again, you might see someone slip and tumble down the rocks to their death. It's a good way to ruin your trip—and then some.

These easy-to-follow, common sense guidelines make tubing on the Salt River incredibly fun. Taking in the spectacular scenery, enjoying the cool water, and meeting plenty of new "river rat" friends make this short trip well worth it. If you find that the summer heat is hard to handle and you need to get away, tubing is a cheap, easy, and enjoyable escape. Pack on the fun and pack out your trash.

Directions

From Phoenix follow Hwy 202 east to Hwy 87 (Beeline Highway). Drive north for approximately 15 miles. Look for the sign for Saguaro Lake and the Lower Salt River Recreation Area. Turn right on the Bush Highway and go 10 miles to the four-way stop at Usery Pass Road. You will see the parking lot on the right.

Outfitters

Salt River Tubing, 480/984-3305, www.saltrivertubing.com

For More Information

U.S. Forest Service, Tonto National Forest, Phoenix, AZ, 602/225-5200

Recommended Reading

Phillips, Steven. *A Natural History of the Sonoran Desert.*
Berkeley, CA: University of California Press, 1999.
Quinn, Meg. *Wildflowers of the Desert Southwest.*
Tucson, AZ: Rio Nuevo Publishers, 2000.

Rafting the Colorado River

America's Grandest Adventure

Easy
$250-$500⁺

Have you ever rowed a boat on a sunny, calm day, on a glasslike lake,
using only one arm the whole time?
> *It gets tiring after a pretty short while.*
Ever try the same one-armed rowing stunt on a river with a current?
> *That gets worse even quicker.*
How about through some of the cruelest, hardest running rapids on earth?

In the summer of 1869, John Wesley Powell, a one-armed Civil War veteran, led the first expedition down the Colorado River through the Grand Canyon. People on river trips today occasionally suggest that the voyage would not have been too difficult even in the

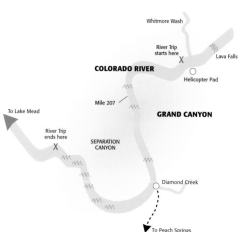

open wooden dories. However, when Major Powell first explored the river, dams did not regulate the water levels. Based on geologic studies and Powell's own book, the virtually unrunnable torrents may have been five to ten times the size of today's rapids. Now Glen Canyon Dam controls the flows, making it hard to imagine what the past was like. As you comfortably cruise down the river, try to imagine Powell's adventure—to get an even start, simply toss your boat guides overboard, cut your boat in half, and at least triple the size of the rapids.

Now that you have an excellent mental picture of Powell's journey, you'll want to find an outfitter to help you create your own rafting adventure. Unfortunately, with all the companies out there clamoring for your business, this task is not as easy as it might seem. *Sorry sir, we're already sold out this year, and actually, more than half of next year's trips are full, too.* This is a likely response when trying to arrange a last-minute Colorado River trip. It does not matter if you are looking for a two-day or a two-week adventure, chances are, unless you are planning well ahead, everything will be booked. Do not despair, but do start planning well in advance. There are only so many permits available, and since whitewater rafting through the Grand Canyon is generally considered America's top adventure, only those willing to plan a little further in advance will be able to experience this breathtaking escape.

"Our longer trips fill up faster than the 3-day trips, but I would still recommend reserving at least seven to eight months prior," said Marcie Clark of Tour West, one of the river's premier rafting operations. "The tighter your schedule is, the farther in advance your reservations should be made." We thought for a moment to ask if anything was open two years down the road to be certain we could get in, but she assured me that with flexible dates and a smaller group, you're more likely to be able to reserve a summer excursion as late as even March. However, this is definitely not guaranteed so to ensure the best trip, start planning at least a year in advance.

Take advantage of this long lead time, and make sure to plan your trip dates well. Weather can make or break your enjoyment level on a vacation such as this. In general, consistent water flows and exciting rapids can be found throughout the season, but the most enjoyable weather is often during the shoulder months of April, May, and September. While the water temperatures hover below 50° F year round, the daytime sun can easily scorch the air temperatures to twice that. Swimming is not recommended in the Colorado River, but popular short hikes lead to waterfalls, which provide refreshing natural showers. Generally during the shoulder months, as an added bonus, you'll find the best deals and encounter fewer people on the river.

Once you have booked a trip, the outfitter will provide you with more information, including a list of items to remember. A wide brimmed hat and strong sunscreen are a must. Despite the rock walls looming over you, towering a vertical mile up from the river, their shade and the splashing water from the rapids cannot alone combat the intense summer sun. If you have any special requirements or dietary considerations, let the company know in advance. They all have worked with so many people over so many years, that even if your request seems strange and impossible, it will be handled with the utmost ease. Water and other drinks are provided, however, you can bring along reasonable amounts of beer or alcoholic beverages. And if you like to fish, talk to your outfitter about the possibilities of fishing on your trip, but purchasing the necessary licenses and stamps will be your responsibility.

For storing your gear, a waterproof duffel bag is provided. For moisture sensitive equipment, an ammo can is issued to each participant, as are tough plastic bags. Many people bring along disposable waterproof cameras for simplicity's sake, but the smaller video cameras are becoming more popular. If you have any questions about taking or caring for your gear on the river, these outfitters will have your answers. Many companies work with movie crews and professional photographers several times a season, so they really know how to take care of gear.

Courtesy of Tour West

Courtesy of Tour West

They also know the river, and the best ways for you to get on it. Most of the three-day rafting trips originate in Las Vegas, which is only a short flight from Arizona. Most tour outfitters do not arrange airfares, but they are abreast of the best fares. From the airport, a short plane ride brings you to the Bar 10 landing strip. Shortly afterwards, a helicopter whisks you to the bottom of the canyon. The river guides graciously welcome you to their watery world and explain what you are about to partake in. With wondrous electricity flowing about the group, most people are in a mild state of shock during this briefing, so the guides make it a point that you understand the safety issues. The trips are usually very safe, but with river running, like any adventure, there are inherent dangers. John Becker of Western River Expeditions warns that although their safety record is excellent and their guides are highly skilled and experienced, a few guests have had minor scrapes or sprains. "The time spent off the river hiking and exploring is a very unique experience, but precautions must be taken. More people get hurt on shore than on the boats." The extracurricular activities are of course up to you as it your vacation, but the magnificent scenery and geology compels you to carefully enjoy your surroundings.

These shorter trips allow you to truly sit back and enjoy the ride. Instead of paddling, a guide masterfully maneuvers the craft with an outboard motor, its purr drowned out by the rushing water and your excitement. The rafts used are stable and spacious enough to allow you to move around during the smoother stretches, chat with the other guests, and take plenty of photos. Likewise, they are comfortable enough for you to effortlessly enjoy the scenery.

Just when you think you might fall asleep because you are so relaxed, your guide warns everyone that the next stretch of whitewater is coming up. The guide warns that this one, rated a solid 5, will be fun. Opposed to the more common Class I through VI whitewater river ratings, the rapids through the Grand Canyon are instead rated on a different scale, ranging from a relaxed 1 to a *white-knuckled, am I gonna die?* 10. Although the lower section of the Colorado River presents a calmer mood for the three-day trips, there is certainly no shortage of thrill as you and your boatload of new friends barrel through rapids rated as high as 6. Even on your first day out, not too long after the orientation, the bubbling whitewater torrents found at the Kolb and Mile 207 rapids plunge you right into the action.

On the morning of the third day, you and the others are transferred to a jet boat and cover the last 35 miles maneuvering the upper stretches of Lake Mead. Although the

Courtesy of Arizona River Runners

majority of the largest rapids are located above Lava Falls and only available on longer trips, the three-day program covers almost 100 miles and provides a breathtaking introduction to river running as well as a chance to sleep under the stars and sample exquisite outdoor cooking. At the trip's end, a bus will shuttle your group back to Las Vegas. When you go, notice the smiles and expressions on the faces of the others. After this weekend escape, the people on that bus are the happiest group in the world.

Directions

Most of the shorter rafting trips start from Las Vegas. Contact your outfitter for details as well as assistance on travel arrangements.

Outfitters

Arizona River Runners, Phoenix, AZ, 800/477-7238, www.raftarizona.com
Canyoneers, Flagstaff, AZ, 800/525-0924, 928/526-0924, www.canyoneers.com
Grand Canyon River Runners, Hualapai Reservations, 888/255-9550
   www.river-runners.com
Tour West, Orem, UT, 800/453-9107, www.twriver.com
Western River Expeditions, Salt Lake City, UT, 800/453-7450, www.westernriver.com

Recommended Reading

Powell, John. *The Exploration of the Colorado River and Its Canyons.*
   New York, NY: Viking Penguin, 1997.
Ryan, Kathleen Jo. *Writing Down the River: Into the Heart of the Grand Canyon.*
   Flagstaff, AZ: Northland Publishing, 1998.
Whitney, Stephen. *A Field Guide to the Grand Canyon.*
   Seattle, WA: The Mountaineers, 1996.

59

16 Houseboating Lake Powell

Home Sweet Boat

Easy
$250-$500⁺

There are few things more relaxing than a houseboat vacation. First, you're at the mercy of no one. There is no need to go back to the hotel to get ready for the evening's activities after a day on the water; no loud upstairs neighbors stomping around at 3 a.m.; and no pushy cleaning personnel knocking too early for comfort. For the duration of your stay, you get to go where you want and take your home away from home with you. For just a little while, you are the ruler of the realm, and you can let your sense of exploration take over completely without having to "rough it" too much.

If this sounds like the best of all worlds, it is. And if you're looking for a place to enjoy this kind of independent-minded escape, look no further than Lake Powell, located on the Arizona-Utah border. This man-made lake is Arizona's best houseboating location and the water gateway into Glen Canyon National Recreation Area. It's a breathtaking example of the desert's natural forces at work and proof of Arizona's amazing beauty.

Lake Powell is a firmly established tourist area that attracts over 3.5 million people per year. It is, however, the subject of some controversy, especially among environmentalists and politicians. The lake was created in 1963 when the Glen Canyon Dam was completed on the Colorado River. Today, Lake Powell is the second largest man-made body of water in the nation, measuring 187 miles in length and offering over 1900 miles of coastline to explore. The creation of the lake stirred controversy at the time, because it flooded large swaths of the Glen Canyon network. In addition, environmentalists maintain that the damming of the Colorado River changed habitats downstream that resulted in the death

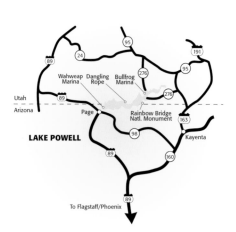

of riverside flora and the extinction of three of the river's eight native fish species. Today, groups like the Sierra Club are still pushing to have the lake drained, and the conflict doesn't show any signs of a compromise. So be aware—if you feel very strongly about environmental issues, you may want to read up on Lake Powell and its history before setting out for it. There are strong arguments on both sides of the issue, so do your homework and decide for yourself whether or not you would feel comfortable vacationing here.

One thing is certain—the creation of the lake did not hamper the natural beauty of the rock formations that lie in and around it. There are 96 large side canyons to explore, and each one offers amazing colors and rock patterns that are guaranteed to astound you. The cliffs rise straight out of the water and shoot up to the sky, often creating a feeling of enclosure in the more narrow canyons. The feeling of chugging through desert formations such as these on the deck of a boat, in an environment where no body of water this big could possibly exist, is alone well worth the trip.

The best way to houseboat is to go with a large group. Most of the boats available for rent on Lake Powell sleep at least six people; the more expensive and glitzy boats can accommodate ten or twelve guests. If you round up a group of friends or family to come along, you'll end up getting a pretty good deal, even on the more plush boats. Rentals

run from a few hundred dollars to over $3000 for three days, so there's quite a bit of latitude in cost; but three grand split between ten people for three days' worth of fun and luxury suddenly doesn't seem quite so pricey. And, as they say, the more the merrier!

But rest assured that you get what you pay for on Lake Powell's houseboats, particularly at the higher end. The Admiral class boats (the highest-priced models) include such amenities as CD audio systems, gas grills, central heating and air, plus luxurious interiors that make you feel like someone took their rich uncle's beachfront condo and stuck pontoons on it. If you've got the funds, go for the gusto; but whichever boat you choose, you'll be comfortable. Each houseboat includes the essentials you need to have a civilized experience among the primal canyons.

There is plenty to do besides float around in your weekend home, though. The fishing in Lake Powell is excellent as you might guess from the number of nooks and crannies all around you. Walleyes, large and smallmouth bass, catfish, and bluegills all populate the depths of Lake Powell—and you know in a body of water this big, you're bound to find some big fins. The hefty striped bass introduced to Lake Powell in the 1960s have delighted anglers ever since. There is also plenty of shoreline to explore, and the lake is great for swimming. Find your own little canyon, drop anchor, and you've got your own private fishing/swimming hole. If the houseboat is a little on the slow side for your adventuring tastes, there are powerboat rentals to lend a little speed to your meanderings.

Be sure to get a little taste of dry land in the Glen Canyon National Recreation Area, too. It's twice as big as Rhode Island, and a great place for backwoods hiking. There are few established trails here, but the sheer size of the area makes the possibilities for exploration and discovery almost endless. Imagine winding your way through the rocks and finding your own closed-in pocket of canyon, something right out of every Southwestern dream.

There are also landmarks worth seeing in the trackless wilderness. Defiance House is a prehistoric Pueblo site in Forgotten Canyon, and a well-preserved reminder of the culture that colonized these canyons long before the American era. The ancient dwelling is one of three open archaeological sites within the Glen Canyon area, and an extensive

Photograph by Ray Bangs

renovation has just been completed on it. Forbidding Canyon is home to the amazing Rainbow Bridge, the world's largest natural bridge, which stands 290 feet above the ground. This formation in particular is worth seeking out; it is awe-inspiring and will haunt you long after your return home. Don't miss it.

Though your houseboat will serve as your base of operations on Lake Powell, your adventure is by no means limited to deck-sitting and burger-flipping. Use your home on the water to give you the freedom to explore this amazing and controversial place. At some point in the future, those who are calling for the draining of the lake may win out, and this adventure will be replaced by those created by the draining. But until then, the only limits on your exploration are the silent canyon walls that hold you in.

Directions

Lake Powell is located near Page, AZ. To reach Page, take I-17 north until you reach the exit for I-40 east (just south of Flagstaff). From there it's a short hop to the US-89 north exit. Stay on 89 for about 128 miles, until you reach AZ-98. From there, you will have access to all areas of the Glen Canyon National Recreation Area and Lake Powell. Talk to your reservations agent about the exact location of your boat's marina, as there are a few different locations around the lake from which to launch. Some are located over a hundred miles past Page across the Utah border, so be sure to inform the agent that you are coming from Arizona. They will help you to cut down on your driving time as much as they can.

For More Information

Glen Canyon National Recreation Area, 928/608-6404, www.nps.gov/glca
Lake Powell Reservations, 800/528-6154, www.lakepowell.com

Recommended Reading

Farmer, Jared. *Glen Canyon Dammed: Inventing Lake Powell and the Canyon Country.*
    Tucson, AZ: University of Arizona Press, 1999.
Kelsey, Michael R. *Boater's Guide to Lake Powell: Featuring Hiking, Camping, Geology,*
    History, & Archaeology. Provo, UT: Kelsey Publishing, 1996.
Martin, Russel. *A Story That Stands Like a Dam: Glen Canyon and the Struggle for*
    the Soul of the West. New York, NY: Holt, 1989.
Wing, Charlie. *The Liveaboard Report: A Boat Dweller's Guide to What Works*
    and What Doesn't. New York, NY: McGraw-Hill, 1997.

Cross the Border to Mexico

Tans, Tacos, and Tequila in Puerto Peñasco

Easy
$0-$500+

The two most important rules when driving into Mexico are first, to purchase good Mexican auto insurance and second, do not try to smuggle anything illegal into or out of the country. Ignoring either of these rules is like asking to be tossed into jail for life. When crossing the border, you'll likely be stopped and searched for smuggled drugs, guns, or American products intended for sale, and the border officials will ask to see your vehicle documents. We highly recommend bringing a passport, (remember that it is another county!) but you can usually get by with a valid Arizona driver's license. Other than your initial border crossing anxiety, you'll have no problems if you proceed with normal caution and maintain respect for the people, culture, and country you are visiting. Sixty more miles and you'll be forgetting about routines, losing your watch, ordering cold margaritas, and having fun!

Puerto Peñasco, or known by us *gringos* as Rocky Point, is Arizona's closest ocean beach resort, located on the northern shore of the Sea of Cortez (Gulf of California), in the state of Sonora, Mexico. Once you cross the border, keep an eye out for the two sometimes easy-to-miss turns in Sonoyta, but signs will accompany you the entire way. If your vehicle breaks down along the Mexican freeway, raise your hood to signal your need for help, and a bright green utility truck will stop to offer assistance. Known as "Green Angels," their job is to help motorists in distress, a free service provided by the Mexican Ministry of Tourism. They can make minor repairs to your vehicle, and you only have to pay for parts. If they do help you, a tip of at least $5 per person is highly recommended.

Rocky Point started as a small fishing village in the 1930s but gradually developed into a major shrimping area. During the U.S. Prohibition era, American entrepreneur Johnny Stone visited the small community and immediately recognized the tourism potential

Photograph by Mary Weil

Photograph by Mary Weil

with its pristine beaches and sunny weather almost year round. Stone built Rocky Point's first hotel and attracted many wealthy Americans to this perfect climate for gambling, drinking, and deep-sea fishing. Even the famous gangster Al Capone was among his original clientele.

Today, Puerto Peñasco is an incredibly popular escape from Arizona. Every weekend, thousands of vacationers embark on the four-hour drive from Phoenix and Tucson, so you can expect the holiday weekends, college spring breaks, and numerous fiestas to be especially busy. With eight RV parks and various camping options, accommodations start at very reasonable rates. If you prefer a little more luxury, you can also choose to stay at the newer hotels or condominiums for a slightly higher rate. And although reservations for any of the accommodations are usually not required, they are highly recommended. So check in, sit back, listen to the mariachi music drift in through the open window, and realize this is what your weekend escape is all about.

With the Sonoran desert on one side and the Sea of Cortez on the other, Rocky Point is a prime place for adventure. The unique ocean conditions produce extreme variances of 25 feet between high and low tides, so do not park on the beach, especially overnight. Swimming in the ocean here, however, is very safe and similar to a calm lake with no rip tides. Rocky Point is also very popular for snorkeling and SCUBA diving. For other active options, you can rent a boat or Jet Skis, and beachcombing the sand dunes of the Altar Desert on an ATV is also fun. If you do rent equipment, be sure to obtain insurance so you do not find yourself in trouble in case of damage. Just out of town, you can explore the interesting terrain of the Pinacate Mountains, which attracted NASA as a training site for their astronauts. And if you're interested in marine life, visit the Intercultural Center for the Study of Deserts and Oceans to view the 55-foot long whale skeleton at the entrance.

Parasailing, windsurfing, and sailing are also common water sports, but the excellent sport fishing attracts the most visitors. Trophy sailfish and marlin are the favorite game fish from June to November, but others pursue the Dorado, better known as Mahi-Mahi, and considered by many as the best fighter. In addition to their beautiful coloring and the nonstop acrobatic action when you hook one, Dorado also have an excellent taste. Their season is shorter though, with peaks in June, October, and November. In addition, various species of sharks are caught year round. Dozens of charter operations advertise their services and guarantee good catches. The quality and extras vary, but the fishing is generally great. If you don't want to hire a boat, follow the examples of others for the shore fishing options. Or, if you just want to bring some fish back to the condo for dinner, the fresh catch of the day can be found at all the local fish markets.

In Rocky Point, Spanish is the official language, but English is widely understood. The Mexican people are proud of their heritage and culture, and will appreciate you trying to speak their language, even if you butcher it. One of the most important words to take with you, though, is a hearty *gracias* (thank you), used whenever possible. Also, dollars

are widely accepted, so don't worry too much about converting your dollars into pesos.

Getting people to agree on the best Mexican food restaurant is difficult, as Rocky Point has plenty of winners. Costa Brava, JJ's Cantina, and the Happy Frog are just a sampling of Rocky Point favorites. From the smallest beachside taco stand to the fancy, gourmet restaurants, they all take pride in the quality and freshness of their food. Lunch is the main meal of the day, but most restaurants stay open fairly late. Drinking bottled water is still recommended, and remember not to drink tap water or use it to brush your teeth, even if it's supposedly filtered. If necessary, over the counter medication is readily available.

With miles of beaches to explore, Rocky Point offers everything from sunsets and *cervezas* at the beachfront cantinas, to souvenir shopping in the local *mercado*, to active sports of all kinds. Whatever you want to do, Rocky Point offers plenty of options for escape into a different country and culture. If you haven't crossed the border yet, it's definitely time to go.

Directions

From Phoenix take I-10 west to Hwy 85 south. Follow Hwy 85 south through Gila Bend and to the border crossing at Sonoyta. Follow the signs to Pto. Peñasco. From Tucson take I-10 to I-19 south. After only a mile, exit onto Hwy 86, also know as the Ajo Highway. Follow Hwy 86 for a little more than two hours to the tiny town of Why. Take a left on Hwy 85 and take that to the border crossing at Sonoyta. Follow the signs to Pto. Peñasco.

For More Information

Green Angels, Toll free number 91-800-903-0092 (in Mexico only)
Santiago Ocean Services, Rocky Point, Mexico, 011-52-6383-58-34 (from U.S.)
   3-58-34 (local in Mexico), www.penasco.com/parasail.html

Returning to Arizona

U.S. Customs & Immigration stops every vehicle to ask questions about your citizenship and the contents of your car. The U.S. Customs Port Director allows citizens to bring back to Arizona $400 in souvenirs per person and 50 lbs. of food per carload (for personal use). Each person over 21 may bring back one liter of alcohol. If you have any questions about what you are bringing back, just ask the border police before you cross. For updates, check their website at: www.customs.ustreas.gov.

Recommended Reading

Kershul, Kris. *Spanish in 10 Minutes a Day.* Seattle, WA: Bilingual Books, 1997.
Weil, Mary. *The Rocky Point Gringo Guide: Puerto Peñasco and Mexico.*
   Tempe, AZ: Frontier Travel Adventures, 1997.

Phoenix Rodeo, Courtesy of Greater Phoenix Convention and Visitors Bureau, Justin Associates, Inc.

World's Oldest Rodeo

Get Along Little Doggies!

Easy
$0–$100 · 1 Day
$100–$500 · 3 Days

In 1884, a group of Arizona ranchers gathered together to celebrate the precious August down time that came before the fall roundup. They met up in northern Gila County, near the town of Payson, to compare their skills in the rancher's arts: roping, riding, and holding on to the back of an angry, bucking bull for as long as humanly possible. The event was called August Doin's, and on that day, an Arizona tradition was born.

The year 2001 marked the 117th anniversary of the World's Oldest Continuous Rodeo, which is the modern descendant of that first gathering in August 1884. The rodeo is no local picnic anymore, though; the Professional Rodeo Cowboys' Association sanctions the event, and that organization has voted the Payson Rodeo as the country's Best Small Rodeo. Every third week in August, competitors from across the nation gather in Payson and are hell-bent on capturing their share of the prize money up for grabs. And, lucky people that we are, we get to watch.

The World's Oldest Continuous Rodeo is a hallowed piece of Arizona's culture and history. The Old West runs hidden through the fabric of life here, and if not for that wild earlier time, Phoenix and Tucson would be as cultureless as McDonald's. While touristy destinations like Tombstone recreate the era through artifice and imitation, the Payson Rodeo gives you the real deal. Everyone knows that cowboys shaped the West, and the Rodeo is a hearkening back to their glory days. It was a time when the most valuable employees in Arizona weren't IT professionals, but people who could sit on a galloping horse and still throw a four-foot loop of rope around the neck of a small, running cow.

In 1882, the famous Buffalo Bill Cody created the standard for competitive rodeos by convincing local merchants to reward top participants with prizes. The Old Glory Blowout of North Platte, Nebraska was the result, and the rodeo has been increasing in popularity ever since. Today, cowboys compete for purses totaling over $25 million in rodeos scattered throughout the West to indoor events held in the friendly confines of New York's Madison Square Garden. In 1996, over 46 million people bought tickets to a rodeo, making it the third most popular live sporting event in the country. The rodeo combines all of the attributes Americans like in their sports: danger, a bit of violence, an interesting cast of characters, and a high level of professional skill on the part of the riding and roping participants.

Although rodeos are sporting events first and foremost, don't think of the Payson Rodeo as a football game or a wrestling match with bulls. It entails much more—parades, pageants, and fairs give the affair the appearance of a festival rather than a couple of hours given over to deciding who is the best wrangler. The clowns alone lend a carnival-like air to the proceedings, as if to say that even with all the action transpiring in the dirt arena, it's nothing to take too seriously.

The Payson Rodeo is usually a three-day celebration, in which both men and women are encouraged to compete and show their skills in the rodeo ring. The whole weekend is complete with an old-fashioned Western parade, rodeo breakfast, and exhibitions alongside the competitive events. The Rodeo starts on Friday night, runs all day Saturday, and wraps up Sunday afternoon. If you cannot stay for the whole three days, don't feel shorted; even one afternoon is plenty of time to catch enough rodeo to make you plan on staying an extra day next year. Be aware that you must pay a small fee to get into the rodeo each

Photograph by Dennis Fendler

day, so if you do decide to stay for a few days, make sure you budget accordingly. Also, if you miss the Payson Rodeo, don't give yourself the spurs; you'll find dozens of rodeos throughout the state from Scottsdale's Parada Del Sol to the Phoenix Rodeo to Tucson's Desert Thunder.

The Payson festival also features dances on Friday and Saturday nights and church in the arena on Sunday morning. The whole affair is a classic "fun for the whole family" event, and the presence of so many horses to pet will make your little ones jump for joy. Buy a bag of carrots to parcel out to the lesser-heralded athletes.

Many people just go to Payson for the rodeo, but there's much more to this area than first meets the eye. Payson is a beautiful little town located in the middle of 3 million acres of forest, which includes the world's largest stand of ponderosa pine. The weather is pleasant year-round, making the August rodeo a perfect escape for those seeking to avoid

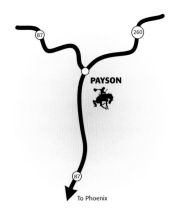

the desert heat plaguing much of the state at that time of year. The whole region in which Payson sits is known as "Rim Country" because of its close proximity to the Mogollon Rim, one of the state's most prominent geographical features. The nearby White Mountains give outdoor buffs a certified paradise in which to play; hikers and bikers of all skill levels will find a plethora of trails and backcountry haunts to wear out their boots and tires on.

There are more urban pursuits to enjoy as well. Mazatzal Casino is located at the south end of Payson on the Beeline Highway. It sits on Tonto Apache land, and lends its sponsorship to the Rodeo. Arizona casinos offer a huge variety of slot machines, automated blackjack and roulette, and card room poker (the only dealer-led table you'll find in Arizona's gaming houses). It's not quite Las Vegas, but it's a pleasant diversion for those of us with the gambling bug. The casino doesn't have hotel facilities, however, so be sure and make arrangements with one located nearby. After all, the Rodeo takes place right across the street.

The World's Oldest Continuous Rodeo is an Arizona adventure that hits on all kinds of levels. It is one part history, one part sport, and two parts Western culture, mixed with a healthy dose of neighborliness and the feeling that you're doing something new. Particularly for the city-bound among us, the Payson Rodeo is a chance to escape to a place we may not know yet, a living part of the culture that defines our state's past. For those of you visiting from around the country and the world, the Rodeo is a perfect stepping-off point to experience the reality of the West. The rodeo, with all of its action and energy, is the living and real soul of Western culture; it captures a reality that artificial gunfights put on by actors cannot. This adventure is enough to make a cowpoke out of anyone.

Directions

To Payson from Phoenix take I-10 East to US-60, exit 154. Head east on 60 until you reach AZ Route 87, also known as the Beeline Highway. Take this north about 65 miles, and you'll reach the Mazatzal Casino and the rodeo grounds across the street. Everything is well marked once you get into the Payson area.

For More Information

Mazatzal Casino, Payson, AZ, 800/777-7529, www.777play.com
Professional Rodeo Cowboys Association, www.prorodeo.com
Rim Country Regional Chamber of Commerce, Payson, AZ, 800/672-9766
   www.rimcountrychamber.com

Recommended Reading

Annerino, John. *Roughstock: The Toughest Events in Rodeo.*
   New York, NY: Four Halls Eight Windows, 2000.
Ehringer, Gavin & Wooden, Wayne S. *Rodeo in America: Wranglers, Roughstock, & Paydirt.*
   Lawrence, KS: University Press of Kansas, 1999.
Santos, Kendra (ed.). *Ring of Fire: The Guts and Glory of the Professional
   Bull Riding Tour.* Chicago, IL: Triumph Books, 2000.

Lake Pleasant Parasailing
Waterskiing Through the Clouds

You are free falling, soaring through the air. You pull your parachute cord, and feel the giant balloon suddenly fill with air. Now you can just float on the gentle currents, look out over the endless horizon, and feel the sun warm your windblown skin…Cut! Hold on a second.

Hang gliding, parachuting, and skydiving are all excellent ways to feel like a bird, but each of them also requires a bit of the daredevil instinct, as well as varying degrees of physical ability. Not just anybody has the prowess, or let's face it, the sheer guts to step out the door of an airplane. Flight-related adventures are, for the most part, not good for children or older folks either, which leaves many people stuck on the ground with clipped wings.

Luckily, Desert Sky Parasailing has an answer for everyone, including both hardcore adventurers and those unable to engage in more extreme flight adventures for whatever reason they might have. Located an hour outside of Phoenix at Lake Pleasant, Arizona's second largest lake, Desert Sky provides the means for the young and old, the brave and yella, to soar with the eagles.

"It's one of the most mellow, low-impact activities you can do," says Don Fraser, owner of Desert Sky Parasailing and Vice President of the World Parasail Boatowners' Association. "I've had people from two to eighty-nine years old go up, and all of them get a big kick out of it. Some get a little scared at first, but it really is the closest most of us can come to flying like a bird."

Parasailing was invented in 1961 in France, when some aspiring parachutists got the bright idea to tie a guy with a parachute to the back of a car and start driving. Sure enough, the chute rose into the air, but they soon discovered that landings on land

resulted in a lot of broken bones. Early parasailers quickly moved to the beach, where they relied on boats to pull them along. Unfortunately, this didn't work out so well either; landings on the water without a means to guide the parasails caused more than a few drownings.

Luckily, by the 1970s, the sport's proponents, led by inventor and parasailing forefather Mark McCulloh, had perfected a guidance system consisting of a large boat fitted with a hydraulic winch. This "winchboat" is the most popular system around today, and the one Desert Sky uses. You strap on a fairly comfy harness while the crew inflates your canopy; then, after you're strapped in and the boat picks up a little speed, you start

Photograph by Danielle Becker

Photograph by Danielle Becker

to gain altitude. When you get to the top, the winchboat simply takes you for a ride, and you can relax at the end of your rope—no steering necessary. The ride lasts between ten and twenty minutes, which gives you plenty of time to feel like a falcon and to snap some quality pictures of those little dots on the ground you came with.

Don's experience and concentration on safety are very important, as parasailing, like any sport, is dangerous without the proper attention. Flying in bad weather is a big no-no, as is flying over land. Desert Sky's creed is safety first, and Don is the only parasailing outfitter in Arizona licensed by the state. He's looking to expand in the future, but at the moment Lake Pleasant is the place to go for maximum fun.

It is also nice to know that Desert Sky has never had any sort of accident. The World Parasail Boatowners' Association is a nationwide group that creates voluntary guidelines for safety—limited altitudes, prohibitions of flying over land, rope regulations—that legitimate providers choose to follow. As the Vice President and a long-time member of this association, you know that Desert Sky and Don Fraser are going to keep you as safe as possible during your adventure and take no chances should conditions not be just right for flying. Luckily, Desert Sky's close proximity to the Valley of the Sun provides plenty of great days throughout the whole season (mid-February to early November).

At Lake Pleasant, you can choose to fly on 500, 700, or 900 feet of rope, depending on how long you want your ride to be and at what height you think you'll be comfortable. The 900-foot flight allows for some real soaring; at that altitude, Don lets the parasail drift a little, letting you experience a taste of the floating thrill a skydiver has with the chute already open. Starting at $35 a ride, the whole activity is relatively inexpensive. There are minor price differences, though, based on your preferences ($10 more for the 700-foot rope, $20 more for 900-foot rope), but remember—the longer the rope, the longer the ride.

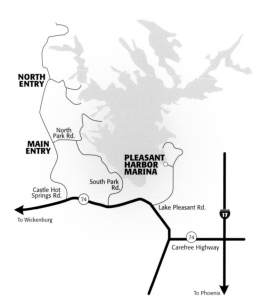

Parasailing is also a perfect family or group activity. For parents who want their kids to experience the amazing feeling of soaring Desert Sky provides a number of options. Toddlers can ride right in mom or dad's arms inside their own harness, while older kids who aren't ready to go it alone can opt for the tandem flight, in which a parent and child can ride up together (Desert Sky doesn't allow adults to ride tandem yet, but Don says that he's looking at picking up a larger chute to make this possible.) It doesn't take all day, so you'll still have plenty of time to enjoy everything else Lake Pleasant has to offer—fishing, camping, and boat rentals, among other things.

There aren't many times in our lives when we get the chance to experience what another creature must feel like. Parasailing is floating in the sky like a hawk, wings extended and rigid, effortless, riding air the way surfboards bounce and cut through waves. It's a quiet and solitude that we don't often get to experience, a time of separation from the earth that lets us think, look around without worrying about pulling a ripcord or steering, and take in the world as it moves along beneath us. It's a feeling all of us should have at least once, whether you're three or eighty, adventurous or timid. Parasailing brings us closer to our dreams of flying.

Directions

From Phoenix to Lake Pleasant (Desert Sky Parasailing is located at the Pleasant Harbor Marina) take I-17 north to Carefree Highway (State Route 74). Then go west 8 miles to Lake Pleasant Road and turn right. The Marina will be on your left; turn in, and Desert Sky is at the front of the docks.

Outfitters

Desert Sky Parasail (see coupon pg 207), Lake Pleasant, AZ, 602/369-0793

For More Information

Lake Pleasant Regional Park, 41835 N. Castle Hot Springs Rd., Morristown, AZ
928/501-1710, www.maricopa.gov/rec_svc/lake_pleasant/#133

Recommended Reading

Krause, Steve. *Streamside Trails; Day Hiking Central Arizona's Lakes, Rivers, and Creeks.*
Tempe, AZ: Pinyon Publishing, 1994.
Will-Harris, Toni. *Hang Gliding and Parasailing (Action Sports).*
Minnetonka, MN: Capstone Press, 1994.

20 Grand Canyon Mule Ride

Hitching a Ride to the River

Medium
$100-$250 · 1 Day
$250-$500 · 2 Days

Have you ever wondered what it would have been like to live in the Old West during the Gold Rush? Imagine sitting on the back of a dusty mule, winding your way down steep trails following sharp drop-offs in search of gold. The summer sun blazes down your back, but a slight breeze keeps you cool. Your entire fate is entrusted to the surefooted steed that carries you and your gear down into the depths of the Grand Canyon…

Well, not much has changed since those times. If you pay attention to the sights and sounds in front of you as you ride down the Bright Angel Trail, you just might feel like you're in another world. Mule riding is one of the rare "new experiences" one can have even if you are an avid outdoor adventurer. These mule rides provide a great opportunity to journey into the Grand Canyon without the hardcore hiking.

Mules are amazing animals. As many people know, they are the offspring of horses and donkeys, and are unable to produce little mules. What they lose in reproductive capability, however, has been given back to them in the form of intelligence, strength, and a powerful streak of self-preservation. Mules are often easier to train than horses, and are three times as strong. Their infamous stubborn disposition is simply their desire to stay alive, rather than to go wherever their human masters direct them. This quality in particular makes them invaluable on the trails of the Canyon, where a bad step can

Courtesy of Arizona Office of Tourism

conceivably put you at the bottom a lot faster than you want to get there.

Don't let the slippery slopes scare you, though; mule rides are a relatively safe way to experience the Canyon. During the past 114 years, over 600,000 people have ridden mules through the Canyon for pleasure, both on the present trails and on a number of now-discarded routes. Captain John Hance began the first business dedicated to mule rides in 1887. Today, Ron Clayton runs the Grand Canyon Mule Operation and averages somewhere around 10,000 customers per year. In all that time, no one has ever perished during a mule ride. A one hundred year perfect safety record should give those of you who are jumpy around heights and/or large animals a good reason to try riding into one of the most scenic areas of the Southwest.

The two-day trip allows you a rare opportunity to venture all the way to the bottom of the chasm, beyond the point where most people get to go. The ride itself is the highlight, though, and even the one-day trip affords you a great sample of the Canyon. It is pointless, really, to try and describe the awe-inspiring scenery of the Grand Canyon as you descend into it; pictures speak louder than words, and first-hand experience is even more powerful. Suffice it to say you will never forget the drops, the sheer walls, or the size and scope of the whole environment. It is something you simply have to experience for yourself, and the mule ride is a unique, relatively low-impact way to do so.

This is not to say, though, that the mules can carry just anybody, or that physical fitness is not important at all. There is a strict set of guidelines you should know about before making reservations. You have to weigh less than 200 pounds fully dressed and be at least 4'7" tall, regardless of previous riding experience. You also need to speak and understand fluent English, and not be pregnant. And despite the fact that the mule does most of the work, you still need to be in pretty good physical shape to handle the ride; hitching a ride on a mule is simply less strenuous, not easy. And as with any Arizona outdoor adventure, proper clothing, a hat, and sunscreen are vital. If you have any questions about other gear you might want to tote along, just ask the outfitter. Of course, don't even think about forgetting the camera.

Once you get there, Phantom Ranch enhances the scenery you've just taken in. Located beside Bright Angel Creek, the Ranch is the only lodging below the Canyon's rim, a little oasis of hospitality. After that long ride, you'll be happy to know that you won't need to eat camp food for dinner, as your package price includes steak (and breakfast the next morning) served by the Ranch staff. You'll probably see some hikers here, too, as Phantom Ranch is a popular way station for them as well. After a few minutes of talking to them, you may start planning your next Canyon descent on foot.

But, since you rode in, chances are you'll ride out too, and with good reason. Climbing out of the Canyon is no joke, and on the return route up the South Kaibab Trail, you'll really start to appreciate the super strength of your trusty steed. Since you're taking a different route, you'll see different scenery, so you might want to conserve some of your film; you wouldn't want to miss capturing another version of the panorama on the way up.

Then, when you've been safely deposited at the top, snap one more frame of your furry friend. He just helped you to experience one of nature's most special gifts in two days, leaving you free from any worries. Give him the honors, and make that shot the one you hang by the fireplace. It'll make your mule proud and serve as a reminder of your trip into another world.

Directions

To get to Bright Angel Lodge from Phoenix, drive north on I-17 to Flagstaff. From downtown Flagstaff turn north on US-180. Continue to the junction of AZ 64. Turn right (north) and proceed to the south entrance of the Grand Canyon National Park. (National Park Service entrance fees apply.) From there, follow the signs to Bright Angel Lodge.

Outfitters

Grand Canyon Mule Rides, 866/646-0388,
www.americanparks.net/grand_canyon_mule.htm

For More Information

Grand Canyon National Park Backcountry Office, Permit Information, 928/638-7875
www.nps.gov/grca (Park Rangers do not take permit requests over the phone.)
Phantom Ranch, AmFac Parks & Resorts, 303/297-2757, www.amfac.com
Recorded Grand Canyon Trail Conditions & Information, 928/638-7888 (24 hr)

Recommended Reading

Anderson, Michael F.; Frazier, Pamela L.; Price, Greer; & Scott, Sandra.
Living at the Edge: Explorers, Exploiters, and Settlers of the Grand Canyon Region.
Grand Canyon, AZ: Grand Canyon Association, 1998.
Stamm, Mike. *The Mule Alternative: The Saddle Mule in the American West.*
Battle Mountain, NV: Medicine Wolf Press, 1993.
Taylor, Karen L. *Grand Canyon's Long-Eared Taxi.*
Grand Canyon, AZ: Grand Canyon Association, 1995.

Lake Havasu Weekender
Arizona's Beach Party

**Medium
$0-$500⁺**

Thanks to MTV, most people now think of Lake Havasu as "that spring break place." The tube shows us thousands of students from Arizona State University to the University of Southern California flocking to the lake for a week of boozy fun in the sun, and in the midst of the hubbub we're tempted to forget that this special oasis is more than just a giant college pool party. Lake Havasu offers something for everyone's tastes, from high-speed Jet-Skiing to family picnicking; that's what makes it one of the best waterfront destinations in the state.

On June 15, 1825, Mayor of London John Garratt laid the first stone of the fifth London Bridge. It was made of granite, and it measured 928 feet in length and 49 feet in width. It was the latest in the line of bridges that had been spanning the Thames River for over 2000 years. Unfortunately, the bridge didn't survive the transition from horses to automobiles for very long. By 1962, the bridge was falling into disrepair, and London officials decided to have a new one built. Always a historically appreciative people, Londoners didn't want to see the bridge, in all its legendary significance and architectural beauty, razed. So, later that year, the bridge went up for sale in a worldwide auction. Question: what does any of this have to do with Arizona? Answer: This mighty bridge stands, stone for stone perfect, over Lake Havasu.

The founder of the town, Robert P. McCulloch, bought the bridge for $2,460,000 in 1968. Over the next three years, he oversaw a massive operation in which every stone was identified by location and was then painstakingly reconstructed in the middle of his twenty-six square miles of land in the Arizona desert. When finished, this magnificent

Courtesy of Lake Havasu Tourism Bureau

Courtesy of Lake Havasu Tourism Bureau

bridge linked the mainland and a large island in the lake. In any case, many of the identifying numbers are still visible on the various stones, so look for them when you cruise up under the bridge on your watercraft of choice.

Whatever your speed, from paddles to double outboards, cruising this historical curiosity is a must. Lake Havasu City is filled with equipment renters and outfitters, over twenty-eight of them. So even if you don't own a Jet Ski, kayak, or fishing boat (and the fish do bite here so bring your rod and reel), gearing yourself up with the right toys should be a snap. If you do own a watercraft, there are marinas and launch points all around the lake, so hook up the trailer. Either way, the bridge along with the cool water it spans will beckon you. You'll probably be glad to spend most of your time on the lake, too; the average temperature is around 108 degrees between June and September, and it's not unusual for the mercury to hit 120. Keeping in and around the water (and especially remembering to drink water) will stop you from evaporating.

Lake Havasu is like a giant Memorial Day picnic, and the more the merrier. If you can gather a group of ten or twelve people to rent a houseboat plus maybe a ski boat complete with skis and wakeboards, you can spend your whole weekend cruising the lake and barbecuing on the deck. If you've got a smaller group or are heading out with the family in tow, houseboat prices are a little steep, but there are onshore accommodations galore. From RV parks to the London Bridge Resort, which is one of the ritzier destinations on the lake, there's a bed to fit every budget. Accommodations mostly come into play during the evenings when the city's nightlife (and your proximity to it) becomes the center of attention; daytimes are all-inclusive, with everyone congregating on Lake Havasu and getting in on the fun.

One of the nicest things about a Lake Havasu adventure is that it's fun for everyone, including families and singles, young and old, as well as the completely social. You're liable to find yourself having a Jet Ski race with the cute guy or girl you saw walking on the beach, or watching your kids make friends while you chat and make your own

Courtesy of Lake Havasu Tourism Bureau

friends with other boaters. It's as close as Arizona gets to beachfront with all the activities and atmosphere that go along with it. Don't be afraid to borrow some mustard from the family grilling burgers next door, and if you're enjoying a beer or two, don't hoard! Your karma will be rewarded in this life or the next.

As you've probably gathered, the lake itself and everything that goes on around it are the major reasons to visit Lake Havasu. But keep in mind that you are in Arizona. As such, there's more than meets the eye to Lake Havasu City. The Sonoran Desert surrounds your oasis, and it's a crime to limit yourself even when the waters gesture with such an appealing invitation. Particularly if you visit Havasu during the winter, there are some great land-based activities well worth looking into. Billy Ray's Hogg Heaven rents Harley Davidsons at very reasonable prices to those who want to get a look at the landscape from the saddle of an iron horse; packages range from $99 for a four-hour tour to over $800 for a weeklong rental. Outback Offroad Adventures also operates out of Lake Havasu and provides eco-friendly tours of the desert complete with informative descriptions of natural and human history of the area.

And let's not forget the more traditional land-based pursuits. Horseback riding and hiking are all within easy reach of Lake Havasu, and they are nice alternatives once you've had your fill of watersports. For golfers, Emerald Canyon Golf Course is a beautiful place to fit in eighteen holes, and the price is reasonable. Lake Havasu City also boasts its share of shopping, as well as a broad selection of restaurants and bars. Every major cuisine is represented, as is every price range. Like the choices at the lake, your dinner possibilities are wide and varied. So remember—even after the sun goes down, there's no reason to turn in early. Just sleep off the rays for an hour or so, make reservations, and enjoy the rest of your evening.

Colorado River

To Kingman

LAKE HAVASU STATE PARK

95

London Bridge Road

LONDON BRIDGE

95

Beach Rd

Beachcomber Blvd

Marina Rd

To Phoenix

Thompson Bay

Colorado River

Lake Havasu is a great weekend escape for everyone, and cost is just as flexible as the activities are. It offers a taste of the beach right here in the desert, but with some important differences. Chances are you'll never have to worry about rain spoiling your plans, nor will jellyfish get into your trunks. And there have never been any records of Great White sightings, tidal waves, or deadly undertow at Lake Havasu. Welcome to the beautiful Arizona beachfront!

Directions

From Phoenix follow I-10 west towards Los Angeles. Turn off at exit 19 (Parker/US-95, Yuma/AZ-95) and take AZ-95 into Lake Havasu.

Outfitters

Arizona's Jet Skis (see coupon pg 207), 888/393-7368, www.arizonawatersports.com
Billy Ray's Hogg Heaven (see coupon pg 207), Lake Havasu City, AZ, 877/464-7933
    www.hoggheavenrentals.com
Emerald Canyon Golf Course, 928/667-3366
Outback Offroad Adventures, 928/680-6151

Houseboat Rentals

Havasu Springs Resort, Parker, AZ, 520/667-3361, www.rentor.com/havasusprings
Sandpoint Marina and RV Park, Lake Havasu City, AZ, 928/855-0549
    www.lakehavasu.com/sandpoint

For More Information

Lake Havasu State Park, 928/855-2784
Lake Havasu Tourism Bureau, 800/242-8278, www.golakehavasu.com

Recommended Reading

Wing, Charlie. *The Liveaboard Report: A Boat Dweller's Guide to What Works
    and What Doesn't.* New York, NY: McGraw-Hill, 1997.

Shangri La Ranch

No More Tan Lines

Medium
$0-$250

In today's society, the media rams all kinds of propaganda about body image down your throat. Advertisements demand that you have a perfect figure and, of course, you can only wear certain clothing styles to cover this well-toned flesh. For the 99% of our population who are not getting calls from the modeling agencies now, and certainly will not be any time soon, the media can be a tough critic of your less than perfect physique. Additionally, clothing is used to make social class distinctions. The more expensive the clothing, the more money the wearer has. But if you put fifty people of varying economic status together in the same room and strip them naked, it would be very difficult to distinguish the millionaire CEO from the minimum wage earner. To many people, body image and clothing are certainly an important part of modern life; however, there is a small but growing minority that have an entirely different view.

How many times have you gone skinny-dipping with others of the opposite sex? According to the American Association for Nude Recreation (AANR), over 40 million Americans have! The thrill of exposure, as well as revealing your body and its imperfections, can be quite exciting, not to mention a big stress relief. For some, it's addictive. Many people "graduate" from skinny-dipping and join a full-fledged nudist organization or club. Even for those who only try it out once, it's a weekend adventure you won't soon forget.

Nudist organizations seem to have a bad reputation, but it is mostly because uninformed people pass rumors and judgment about things they know little or nothing about. The first common misconception is that "nudist colonies" are immoral places where people go to have promiscuous sex. Nudists make a clear distinction between nudity and sex and keep both in their proper perspective. Inappropriate behavior is very rare, but it is quickly reprimanded if it does occur. The second mistaken belief is that only people with stunningly good looks and perfect bodies are nudists; but really, nudists are just regular people from all walks of life and come in all shapes, sizes, colors, and creeds. It is a little surprising, but not entirely uncommon to see a friend, neighbor, or even a business acquaintance at a nudist resort. The third misconception is that nudists just lie around the pool, sipping boat drinks, and working on their tan. While many nudists definitely enjoy a poolside margarita, many of Arizona's nudist clubs are very active with leisure interests such as hiking, horseback riding, beach volleyball, basketball, and tennis. Of course, all without clothes on!

Nudism, or also commonly referred to as naturism, is an opportunity to relax, have fun, and maybe most importantly, forget about social class distinctions as well as body condition, size, or shape. Nudists respect each other's individuality and uniqueness, while at the same time enhancing their own self-esteem and positive body image. By accepting themselves and their imperfections, accepting others is much easier. Becoming more involved with social nudism is most commonly accomplished by joining a club. The two types of naturist clubs are "landed" and "non-landed." A landed club has its own facilities, while a non-landed club often meets at a member's house or travels as a group to a landed club's establishment. Many club members also join others for worldwide nudist cruises and adventure vacations.

The Shangri La Ranch, only 45 minutes from Phoenix, is one of Arizona's biggest and most popular landed clubs. The family- and couples-oriented facility welcomes newcomers

Photograph by Ray Bangs

Photograph by Ray Bangs

to the nudist lifestyle by maintaining a clothing-optional policy, except for when using the pool and spa. The greatest fear of most people new to nudism is walking out to the pool wearing nothing more than their birthday suit only to see everyone else with their clothes on. At the Shangri La Ranch, since just about everyone is nude, the opposite is true. Even upon initially touring the grounds, you'll quickly decide if you're comfortable with the naturist lifestyle and thus, ready to get naked. As you ease into this nude environment, you'll see people relaxing, having fun, and enjoying the desert surroundings, all without clothes on. Here, nudity is the norm.

The social schedule at the Shangri La Ranch can be especially busy on weekends. Theme parties, karaoke, card games, sporting events, and live bands are a sampling of the indoor activities. Cookouts, water volleyball matches, group hikes, and even nude skydiving are popular as well. Besides the myriad of available indoor and outdoor activities, the Shangri La Ranch is also a full-scale resort and recreation destination. While daily visitors can enjoy a day back to nature until the check-out time at dusk, overnight guests will enjoy a variety of lodging options. Accommodations vary from basic motel rooms to deluxe rental units. Larger groups can rent a lodge with three bedrooms, two baths, a full kitchen, a dining room, and a living room with a fireplace. Numerous RV sites with full hookups are available, and tent camping areas are offered for the more adventurous or for those on a budget. Depending on your choice of accommodations, a visit to the Ranch is a very reasonable resort weekend starting as low as $50.

Jardin del Sol, another Arizona landed club, is located in Marana, 90 miles south of Phoenix and 35 miles north of Tucson. Also offering RV sites, camping, and limited lodging, Jardin del Sol strives to promote environmentally friendly recreation. Recycling and minimum impact practices are also stressed. The nudism policy is simply: unclothed when possible, clothed when practical. Visitors can enjoy the hiking and other desert activities as well as the swimming pool and Jacuzzi. Both the Shangri La Ranch and Jardin del Sol are popular stops for non-landed, or travel nudist clubs. Members of AANR and other nudist organizations receive a discount.

Based in Mesa, the Canyon State Naturists is a clothing-optional travel club with a membership of nearly 1000 individuals, who enjoy monthly weekend camping and hiking trips in addition to the yearly four-day house-boating trip on either Lake Mead or

To Flagstaff

New River Rd.

New River

Exit 232

SHANGRI LA RANCH

New River Rd.

7th Avenue

17

Exit 223   Carefree Highway

74

To Phoenix

Lake Powell. A second Phoenix-based travel club is the Arizona Wildflowers, which organizes pool parties, camping trips, potluck dinners, and the occasional weekend-long event. The Buff-A-Teers, a club based in Tucson, holds camping trips in the mountains of southern Arizona as well as excursions to landed resorts both in Arizona and California. Getting involved with a club, landed or not, is an easy way to take off your clothes. If you enjoy the experience, you can join the club and participate more.

If you want to get out and really try something new, try nude. Throwing away body image stereotypes is a great way of getting to know yourself better and even boosting your self-esteem. For your weekend escape, you can enjoy an unclothed hike through the desert, play a game of sand volleyball, or just relax by the pool. It may be difficult to disrobe at first, but since everyone else is naked, going nude just seems natural. If anything, you won't have any tan lines.

Directions

The Shangri La Ranch is located approximately 45 minutes from the Phoenix Sky Harbor International Airport. Follow I-17 north to exit 223. Drive the Carefree Highway four miles east to 7th Avenue. Turn left and drive seven miles north to Shangri La Road. Turn left and drive 1/4 mile to the entrance. All roads are paved.

Landed Clubs/Resorts

Jardin del Sol, Marana, AZ, 520/682-2537 , www.sunnyjds.com
Shangri La Ranch, New River, AZ, 800/465-8760, www.shangrilaranch.com

Travel Clubs

Arizona Wildflowers, Phoenix, AZ , www.azwildflower.com
Buff-A-Teers, Tucson, AZ, 520/293-5854, http://members.aol.com/buffateers
Canyon State Naturists, Mesa, AZ, 480/539-6399 , www.canyonstatenaturists.com

For More Information

American Association for Nude Recreation, 800/Try-Nude, www.aanr.com
Western Sunbathing Association, www.wsanude.com

Recommended Reading

Ableman, Paul. *Beyond Nakedness*. Topanga, CA: Elysium Growth Press, 1996.
Lange, Ed. *Family Naturism in America: A Nudist Pictorial Classic*.
  Newfoundland, NJ: Events Unlimited, 1990.
Lange, Ed. *Fun in the Sun: Nudist and Naturist Living*.
  Newfoundland, NJ: Events Unlimited, 1986.

Photograph by Ray Bangs

Backcountry Fishing
Black River Bronzebacks

Medium
$0–$100

When summer's temperatures are predicted to surpass the 110° F mark, knowledgeable Arizona anglers drive three hours east of Phoenix to cool off in the White Mountains. Stretching through these rugged mountains for nearly 60 miles, the Black River offers outstanding smallmouth bass fishing. Catching 100 of these bronze-backed smallies in one day is possible, while reeling in 40 is easily done. And to think, these bronzebacks have only been in the so-called desert state for less than a century!

The range of the smallmouth bass originally spanned from Minnesota to Quebec, west to Oklahoma, and south to northern Alabama, but the sporting smallie quickly became known as a feisty fighter. As early as the mid-1870s, the U.S. Fish Commission, which eventually helped form the U.S. Fish and Wildlife Service, developed railroad cars that could carry live fish over long distances in order to stock waters far and wide with sport species. Smallmouth bass were frequent passengers, and they were introduced into Arizona in 1921. Arizona anglers have since been quite grateful.

Although found in a variety of waters, smallmouth bass are most frequently found in clear lakes with rocky bottoms and little vegetation. Boulder-strewn streams with large pools providing cover such as overhanging banks, tree roots, and brush are also excellent smallie habitat. Because of these factors, the Black River is generally considered Arizona's best bet for aggressive bronzeback action.

Smallmouth bass are predators, feeding primarily on crayfish, minnows, insects, and the occasional unlucky frog. Dawn and dusk are often the best fishing periods, when the bass are pursuing their favorite food: the nocturnal crayfish. During the rest of the day, the bass frequent the shallow riffles to attack any food drifting past. The most productive lures for Black River smallmouths are plastic worms, streamer flies, and anything resembling minnows, while the best live baits include hellgrammites and crayfish. Many traditional anglers even like to pursue the bass with fly rods.

With an early start, many Arizona anglers make this outing a one-day trip. This is a good option if you don't plan to explore the river too much, but the drive alone can make for a very long day. Most people opt to camp along the river's edge, with the spectacular

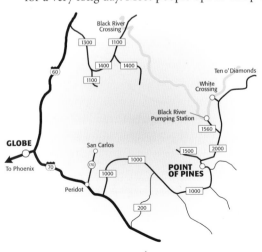

solitude and wilderness adding to the experience. The Black River flows through some of Arizona's most unlikely scenery, including the lush forests reminiscent of the eastern United States. Camping is strictly limited to wilderness sites so make sure to exercise extra caution. Spending the night too close to the river during the summer monsoon season should be avoided, as flash floods are rare, but they are a potentially dangerous threat.

While tourism and advertising campaigns have so successfully heralded Arizona as the desert state, the terrain of the rugged, yet lonely White Mountains offers a good chance of seeing elk, deer, turkeys, javelinas, mountain lions, and even black bears. To reduce the chances of any uninvited, nighttime guests, be sure to keep a clean camp and hang your food. Of course, if these images are a little too wild for you, hotels are available in the nearby towns of Globe and Superior.

Just getting to the Black River can be a challenge. Accessible from the road with a 2WD vehicle, the bridge at Black River Crossing is a very popular spot with several deep pools. However, like with most rivers, the best fishing is not at the most easily reached areas. If you are seeking the solitude of a real backcountry experience, hiking only an hour will offer world-class fishing with a good chance of being the only soul around. Remember that this is tough country, and the chances of encountering a black bear or rattlesnake are much higher. But for those taking precautions and venturing further into this vast wilderness, be assured that even more spectacular fishing opportunities await.

A 4WD vehicle is highly recommended if you are going to follow the rough roads from Port of Pines. You will be rewarded by almost streamside parking for some of the more interesting hot spots. The area by the pumping station receives more pressure, but if you hike downstream just a mile or two, you will find excellent, isolated fishing. The way back to the truck is tough, however, as a staircase with enough steps to rival a Tibetan temple is your last obstacle. Ten o' Diamonds is another spot where you can drive very close to the river's edge. Here, in the transition zone between the cold and warm waters, you might be able to tie into a few brown trout as well. Other popular areas include White Crossing, Elwood Canyon Tank, and Coupon Tank.

Most of the smallies in the Black River are 12 to 14 inches, but the occasional 18-inch fish keeps things exciting. The Black River also boasts some hefty brown and rainbow trout as well as the native Apache trout in the upper sections. The best smallmouth fishing season starts in May, usually peaks in mid to late June, and continues through September. An Arizona fishing license is not necessary, but a Black River Recreation Permit is required. The permit is available at the Express Stop in Globe, and it costs $10 per day. Be sure to ask about camping permits since regulations vary.

Since it is such an adventure just getting to this remote area, many people are discouraged from going any further. Once you're on the water, though, getting the fish to strike is relatively easy. Just remember that if you commit to hiking just one hour up or downstream, your efforts will pay off with better fish and an incredible campsite.

Directions

From Phoenix follow US-60 east to Globe. Take US-70 to Peridot and follow Road 1000 north to Point of Pines. For the Pumping Station, White Crossing, and Ten o' Diamonds, turn onto Road 2000. For Elwood Canyon and Coupon Tank take Road 1500.

Outfitters

Anglers and Hunters Travel (see coupon pg 207), Phoenix, AZ, 800/658-5740
  www.anhtrvl.com
Troutback Flyfishing (see coupon pg 207), Show Low, AZ, 800/903-4092
  www.troutback.com

For More Information

San Carlos Recreation & Wildlife Department, 928/475-2343
  (Call to request the map and visitors guide, plus a list of local guides.)

Photograph by Ray Bangs

U.S. Forest Service, Alpine Ranger District, Apache-Sitgreaves National Forest
602/339-4384
U.S. Geological Survey, Current Stream Flows, http://dg0daztcn.wr.usgs.gov
White Mountain Apache Tribe, Wildlife & Outdoor Recreation Division
www.wmatoutdoors.com

Recommended Reading

Hirsch, Bob. *Outdoors in Arizona : A Guide to Fishing and Hunting.*
Phoenix, AZ: Arizona Highways, 1988.
Meck, Charles & Rohmer, John. *Arizona Trout Streams and Their Hatches:
Fly-Fishing in the High Deserts of Arizona and Western New Mexico.*
Woodstock, VT: Backcountry Publications, 1998.
Sagi, Guy J. *Fishing Arizona: The Guide to Arizona's Best Fishing!*
Phoenix, AZ: Golden West Publishing, 1998.

24 Hang Gliding
Your Own Set of Wings

There are plenty of ways to fly in Arizona, everything from a tow over Lake Pleasant to a 15,000-foot float over the northern reaches of the state in a pillowy paragliding wing. Each of these, in its own way, is a form of aviation simply cut into different shapes. Paragliding is a stately eagle soaring; piloting fighter planes is the pure adrenaline of dueling peregrines; and hot air ballooning is the slow, lazy drift of a condor on the breeze. Hang gliders, if they resemble any member of the avian kingdom, are a lot like

Photograph by Gill Couto

Photograph by Gill Couto

the crane; they are a little unwieldy on the ground, but once in the air, seem born to belong there. Few things in the sky have more grace than a hang glider in flight, and few adventures can take you closer to bridging the gap between the birds and your own ground-stuck self, thanks to the wonders of motorless aviation.

Hang gliding works like this: you hold the glider up and run down an incline until the wind speed reaches 15 or 20 mph. At that point, the momentum of the air moving past you creates lift under the wings, and you take off into the wild blue yonder. If there are no hills, vehicles can tow you up like a big kite, but typically, beginners start off learning how to perform a "foot launch," using no equipment besides their legs, their glider, the land, and the air.

Arizona has a prototypical hang gliding landscape—large mountains surrounded by broad expanses of flat, low land. Another compelling factor for Arizona hang gliding is the optimal weather, as most of the nation's other premier hang gliding spots experience a lot more precipitation and biting cold than we do. In Arizona, a 10,000-foot flight is still fairly comfortable (every 1000 feet drops the temperature roughly four degrees—not bad when ground temps are 114° F), while chillier sites require heavy-duty clothing at that altitude. You don't need a whole lot of wind, either; generally 5-25 mph of standing breeze will suffice. Too much wind will result in dangerous conditions and too little wind will mean no conditions at all!

It is only logical, given our weather and geography, that Arizona is a premier hang gliding destination for Americans and the rest of the world. The result of this popularity is a healthy and helpful hang gliding community in our own backyard. They are a strong presence, and always eager to take new recruits skyward. The foundation of this community is the Arizona Hang Gliding Association (AHGA), an organization based in Phoenix but dedicated to promoting the sport throughout the state. If you are an Arizona native and interested in giving hang gliding a try, or a visitor who happens to be in town at the time, head over to the Peter Piper Pizza by the Metrocenter in central Phoenix on the second Tuesday of the month at 7:30 p.m., and you'll find the AHGA and other people interested in hang gliding gathered to discuss safety, site development, and other issues

Photograph by Gill Couto

dear to pilots' hearts. Don't be afraid to show up if you're just curious; if anyone can direct you to the right instructor, it's the folks at the AHGA. Just pick their brains a little, enjoy some pizza, and listen.

Once you have satisfied your curiosity by meeting the professional pilots, you should take some time and learn a little bit about the giant crane-like beast that will be transporting you through the air. The typical glider measures between 26 and 36 feet in wingspan, and weighs 50 to 75 pounds. Obviously, running around on the ground with one of these things can be a bit awkward. It requires some physical prowess, too; you need to be able to run with your wings balanced above you, and keep the 50-75 pound load from pitching around too much on takeoff. Once you're off the ground, however, great strength is largely unnecessary since your body will hang from the glider. Do be aware, though, that a fair degree of upper-body endurance is necessary for longer trips. You also need to pay attention, as the hang glider moves faster than a paraglider does, requiring a constant clear head and concentration. Fliers should also be extra careful to avoid the kind of accidents that can creep up on any airborne adventurer—exhaustion, heavy wind, bad weather, or even a flock of birds. Be smart, and you'll fly smart. Try to fly like an idiot, and you may get yourself hurt as well as answer your whole family's questions as to just how stupid you can be. It is aviation, and the people who do it are pilots; take it seriously and safely.

While you don't have to have a pilot's license to hang glide, there is a rigorous, standardized training regimen run by the United States Hang Gliding Association (USHGA), dedicated to making sure that people who are just starting out get the best introduction to the sport. The instructors listed in the directory are all certified by the USHGA, and each one offers slightly different programs and prices. When it comes down to it, though, they all break down into essentially the same deals, depending on the time and inclination you have to learn.

The first option is to get acquainted with the whole idea. The best way is to go up in tandem with a professional pilot, along with taking some ground school classes and training on how to take off and land (obviously two very important things in the world of hang gliding). After taking part in this initial training, then you can advance to the Beginner's training level, which is also the first step on the standardized proficiency test. Work at it, and in a few months you may get yourself up to an Advanced level and start taking longer flights—a hang glider is capable of reaching a 15,000 foot altitude and soaring over 300 miles. Just make sure you find a loyal driver to follow you before you get that good!

If you're just visiting, there's no better reason to return to Arizona next year than to come back for the hang gliding. Start earning your wings this week, and come back next year to experience the desert sky again. It's worth braving the summer heat to have a chance to rise above it.

Directions

To get to the Peter Piper Pizza at the Metrocenter Mall, where the AHGA meets the second Tuesday of every month, take I-17 north towards Flagstaff to exit 208, Peoria Avenue. Turn left onto W. Peoria Avenue, and then left onto the North Black Canyon Highway. At Cheryl Drive, take a slight right, then turn right again onto North Metro Parkway Drive. You'll immediately see Peter Piper Pizza; bring any questions along.

Outfitters

Eagle's Flight Hang Gliding School (see coupon pg 209), Phoenix, AZ, 602/504-9289
    www.arizonahanggliding.com
Skymasters School of Hang Gliding (see coupon pg 209), Phoenix, AZ, 623/465-3240
    www.airsportsarizona.com
Soaring Solutions (see coupons pg 209), Chandler, AZ, 480/782-6936
    www.soaring-solutions.com

For More Information

The Arizona Hang Glider Association, www.ahga.org
United States Hang Gliding Association, www.ushga.org

Recommended Reading

Fair, Erik. *Right Stuff for New Hang Glider Pilots.*
    Laguna Beach, CA: Publitec Editions, 1987.
Pagen, Dennis. *Hang Gliding Training Manual: Learning Hang Gliding Skills for
    Beginner to Intermediate Pilots.* Black Mountain, NC: Black Mountain Books, 1995.

SCUBA Diving
Arizona's Underwater World

Difficult
$100-$500+

Amazingly enough, Arizona boasts one of the highest concentrations of SCUBA divers per capita in the United States, and some even claim we are number one. Although it's easy to ask how this can be possible, think about the abundance of Arizona dive sites, our astounding number of dive shops, and our easy access to California and Mexico, and it becomes easier to believe. SCUBA is short for Self Contained Underwater Breathing Apparatus, so yes, just like you see on the Discovery Channel, you will be able to breathe underwater and safely swim with the fish. SCUBA diving is one of the best weekend escapes, because you are not only escaping your everyday routine, but you are also escaping into another world. As a bonus, the SCUBA diving community is one of the most fun-loving, travel-addicted groups you could ever get involved with.

Anyone who is in decent physical shape, can swim fairly well, and is not absolutely terrified of the water can learn to dive. But be aware that diving can range from leisurely swims to very taxing technical dives, so before you put too much effort into your certification, getting a basic doctor's exam is recommended. If you've ever had any ear problems when flying, make sure to mention this as it could cause problems in the water. After being given the okay from your doctor, the first step to becoming a certified diver is to sign up for a Basic Open Water class. There are many certification agencies, but PADI (Professional Association of Diving Instructors) is the largest and is globally recognized, which is important if you want to dive in exotic locales.

The Basic Open Water course PADI offers is divided into three phases and can be completed in two weekends. The three phases are Phase I: Academic (classroom), Phase II: Confined Water (pool), and Phase III: Open Water. Don't be scared off by the word Academic in Phase I; your instructor will help you through every step, and an excellent book detailing the fundamentals of SCUBA is included in the course cost. You should read the book prior to Phase I, because you will review it while in class, watch instructional videos, and then take quizzes on each section, or module. The final exam is nothing to worry too much about, because everything is very understandable and is mostly common sense.

There are several types of SCUBA certification classes available for Phase I & II, which are often packaged together. First is the traditional class where you meet one or two times a week for several hours for a duration of two to six weeks. This is the best way to learn the material as you spend the most time at it, but the time involved is often not practical for many people. The second type of course is an Internet course, where you do all the book lessons, take a written test, and then get

into the pool. The last type of certification class is the weekend or executive class, where you spend approximately eight hours on both Saturday and Sunday reviewing the book material, taking the tests, and completing the pool skills. This works well for those who have a limited amount of time. The average cost of getting certified is $200, plus you will need your own mask, snorkel, fins, and booties. The dive shop you are training with will provide all the other gear for the pool.

Phase II will be your first experience breathing underwater, and without giving away too much of the thrill—it is amazing! Since this Pool Phase is usually packaged with Phase I, many dive shops have pools on site, making the training easy and convenient. In the pool, you will practice all the essential skills needed to dive safely in an Open Water environment.

The final step is Phase III where you must complete four Open Water certification dives out in the ocean or in a local lake. Safety is the main concern. You will practice and be tested on the basic SCUBA skills you learned in class and in the pool, but now in a new, larger scale environment. Of course, don't be surprised if a fish or two wants to investigate your class. Often, this third phase is not included in the original certification cost but most shops offer several options with varying prices. The four dives cannot be completed in just one day so camping trips to a local lake or to Rocky Point are an inexpensive way to earn your Basic Open Water SCUBA Certification, known as a "C-card." You can even receive a referral from your Phase I and II instructor and complete your dives with another PADI professional, which works out nicely if, for instance, you are about to embark on a journey to the Bahamas.

Courtesy of *Southwest Diver Magazine*

After completing the three phases, you are certified and can SCUBA dive (always with a buddy!) just about anywhere in the world. Mail in the signed forms from your instructor plus two passport-sized photos, and within several weeks your C-card will arrive in the mail. The card is good for life, though if you lapse in your diving, you might want to take a refresher course. You will need this card to rent or purchase SCUBA equipment, fill air tanks, or go on dive trips. If you have an immediate trip planned, your instruct can provide a temporary card for you.

Many Arizonans travel all over the world to breathe underwater, but surprisingly, the Grand Canyon State offers a multitude of interesting dive destinations. Smaller local lakes like Saguaro and Roosevelt near Phoenix, the bigger lakes of Havasu and Mead, and even sections of the Colorado River are just a sampling of the more popular dive sites. The diving in Arizona is unique since many of the lakes are dammed rivers, so the terrain is basically that of a flooded canyon. Of course, the lakes and rivers are freshwater, so you won't see coral reefs or exotic fish, but the more you explore Arizona's underwater world, the more likely you'll find yourself swimming by World War II bombers, helicopters, and abandoned automobiles…and that's just the start.

One of the most exciting Arizona dive locations is Lake Havasu. Submerged at the bottom of the lake, you will find an underwater town complete with a saloon, a blacksmith's shop, and a 2-story hotel! Or, if you'd like, bring a dive camera and have your buddy take a photo of you sitting behind the steering wheel of an old, submerged Army jeep. While you are there (especially if it's after college spring break), be sure to check out Copper Canyon; treasure-hunters dive to find sunglasses, watches, and wallets galore! Ask your instructors periodically about some of their favorite dive sites as new ones are discovered frequently.

Although the first two weekend diving escapes are spent learning, when you finally earn your C-card and take that initial experience in the open water, you will be creating moments you won't soon forget. Dozens of specialty ratings and advanced certifications can be earned as you progress. When you are certified, you and your dive buddy can go just about anywhere there is water, and as you become part of the SCUBA community, you will discover that Arizona and the nearby areas have plenty of dive puddles into which you will love to escape.

Directions

In Phoenix, the El Mar Diving Center is located in Mesa on Broadway Road, just east of Hwy 101. In Tucson, Desert Divers has two shops with training available at both. The eastside location is at the northwest corner of Kolb Road and Speedway Avenue, while the westside shop can be found at the southwest corner of River Road and First Ave. In Lake Havasu City, located on McCulloch Boulevard, just west of Acoma Boulevard, AquaStrophics Dive & Travel offers training as well as guided trips to some of Lake Havasu's most interesting dive sites.

Outfitters

AquaStrophics Dive & Travel (see coupon pg 209), 2149 McCulloch Blvd
    Lake Havasu City, AZ, 520/680-3483, www.aquastrophics.com
Desert Divers - East (see coupon pg 209), 1113 North Kolb Rd. Tucson, AZ
    520/290-3483, www.desertdivers.com
Desert Divers - West (see coupon pg 209), 4837 North First Avenue, Tucson, AZ
    520/887-2822, www.desertdivers.com
El Mar Diving Center (see coupon pg 209), 2245 West Broadway Rd., Mesa, AZ
    480/833-2971, www.elmar.com

For More Information

PADI (Professional Association of Diving Instructors), www.padi.com
Southwest Diver Magazine, www.southwestdiver.com

Recommended Reading

Bane, Michael. *Diving on the Edge: A Guide for New Divers.*
    New York, NY: The Lyons Press, 1998.
Graver, Dennis. *SCUBA Diving.* Champaign, IL: Human Kinetics, 1999.
Rossier, Robert. *Dive Like a Pro: 101 Ways to Improve Your Scuba Skills and Safety.*
    Flagstaff, AZ: Best Publishing: 1999.

Paragliding
The Air of Paradise

You're standing there with your wings spread behind you, looking down the hill at ground you won't touch. As you start to run, your wings simultaneously expand, transforming from inert cloth lying on the ground into a billowing nylon canopy. You feel each step getting lighter as you are tugged skyward. Soon the earth is a memory; you gain altitude and the wings feel like your own, ready to carry you anywhere.

The high you're experiencing is paragliding, an adventure for the strong of heart and mind. This adventure is definitely not for everyone, but if you want to experience the meditative life of a majestic falcon in flight, then paragliding is your ticket.

The foremost thing to remember before setting out is to be prepared, both physically and mentally. Physical fitness and coordination are important since just getting off the ground requires toting the wing along behind you and steering it once you get into the air. But strength is clearly secondary to being mentally prepared. As a student, you'll have to think with a clear head, act quickly and intelligently on your instructions, and always be calm and in control. So get a good night's rest beforehand and be ready to listen and learn. Unlike many sports and activities, paragliding is one that doesn't have any easy stepping-stones to prepare you; even pilots and skydivers only have a tiny head start on the complete novice. Learning to paraglide is serious business, a highly advanced activity for serious people.

For some, there's also the matter of height—the average recreational pilot often soars over 10,000 feet in the air, and stays aloft for two or three hours. In the end, it's a judgment call based on how serious your fear of heights is. If you think you can handle being up there, then go for it. But even if you are afraid, don't immediately dismiss paragliding; it may be a good opportunity to conquer this fear. According to Airplay Paragliding School, "launches and landings are slow and gentle and, once in the air, most people are surprised by how quiet and peaceful the experience is. Even a fear of heights is rarely a factor, as there is no sensation of falling." If you follow directions and go in with an open mind, you may just surprise yourself.

A quick word about the weather—it's a big factor in paragliding, as it is in all airborne pursuits. Too much wind or a little rain can transform a safe activity like this one into a deadly gamble. If the weather outside is indeed frightful, chances are your instructors won't let you fly that day. But don't worry; the worst that will happen is that they will send you home and offer to reschedule your excursion. Ask about the weather policy beforehand, so you know what to expect if the clouds roll in at the wrong time.

There are only a few paragliding schools and instructors in Arizona, but the best is Dixon White, who runs Airplay out of Cashmere, Washington and Flagstaff, Arizona. He heads a highly competent staff of teachers, and White personally received the 1999 United States Hang Gliding Association's Instructor of the Year award. You're in good hands here; Dixon has supervised over 19,000 student flights, and he lives for teaching the sport to determined, new enthusiasts. As paragliding requires quite a bit of instruction and has a great potential for danger, it's a good idea to know your instructor before going up. If you decide to go with another company, do your homework, ask lots of questions, and even ask for references. If you don't have the time to call around, though, Airplay is a trustworthy company with a great track record.

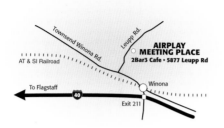

One of the big advantages of going with Airplay is the way they cater to beginners. Their Flagstaff launch site is at 6000 feet above sea level, is beautiful throughout the year, and is nearly perfect during the summer. They've got 600 acres of training ground in Arizona, which allows for plenty of open space for both launching and landing. The Introductory Class takes two days, starting with classroom instruction and the basic mechanics of take-offs and landings. By the end of the first day, you'll already be taking short flights while you get the hang of operating the wing; the second day is filled with solo flights from the training park's Upper Hills. The introductory program is a great way to get acquainted with the sport and your instructor, who will be a valuable asset if you are interested and dedicated enough to pursue paragliding and take further lessons, purchase your own equipment, and make it a lifestyle.

If you do get hooked (which is almost guaranteed), the money you paid for your introductory lesson at Airplay gets applied as credit for the next group of lessons (your Novice certification). You'll also get a discount on equipment when you buy your own. If you decide to pursue paragliding, you'll soon learn that getting your own wing is a good idea, as different people require different attributes in their gear. During your introductory lesson, your instructor will provide you with the right equipment.

Photograph by Phil Schofield

If you still want to try paragliding, but for whatever reason you aren't inclined to do it on your own, Airplay also offers 30-45 minute tandem rides with an instructor. You will be allowed to have some hands-on control of the wing if you want, but you are free to let your pilot do all the flying, too. Be aware, though, that paragliding is not a sport for everyone. Ask yourself if you are really serious about it before committing to your first flight; your life is on the line up there! As a guy who used to ride unicycles on tightropes, Dixon prefers students who are serious about learning all the intricacies needed to fly; he even interviews potential pilots before providing all the instruction. So if you are interested in this thrilling sport, make sure you are aware of all the risks before signing up for even this initial tandem ride.

Flight is one of man's oldest dreams, and paragliding is one of the safest, lowest impact ways to get a taste of the wild blue yonder. It is a peaceful, mind-opening experience, and a great way to join the natural skyscape without all that disrupting noise, speed, or machinery. The only power will come from you, the air, and the environment around you—the hawks off your wingtip, the treetops far below your toes. Take advantage of this opportunity, and enjoy your flight.

Directions

To get to the 2Bar3 Cafe in Flagstaff, where Airplay meets its clients to pick them up and transport them to the launch site, take I-40 east from Flagstaff to Townsend-Winona Road, exit 211. Go left and proceed to Leupp Road. Turn right and drive for 1/2 mile; Airplay's instructors will give you a meeting time when you call to make your reservation.

Outfitters

Airplay Paragliding School and Flight Park, Flagstaff, AZ, 928/526-4579
    www.airplay.com
Alas de Arizona Paragliding School, Tucson, AZ, 520/743-9747
    http://personal.riverusers.com/~bigair

For More Information

The Arizona Hang Glider Association, www.ahga.org
United States Hang Gliding Association, www.ushga.org

Recommended Reading

Cook, Matthew & Sollom, David. *Paragliding—From Beginners to Cross-Country.*
    North Pomfret, VT: Trafalgar Square, 1998.
Pagen, Dennis. *The Art of Paragliding.*
    Spring Mills, PA: Sport Aviation Publications, 2001.
Whittall, Noel. *Paragliding: The Complete Guide.*
    New York, NY: The Lyons Press, 2000.

Fall

Scenic Driving Tours

Arizona's Highways

Half the reason to take any of the adventures offered in this book is to experience our state's incredible scenery. Arizona contains some of the most amazing natural landmarks in the country, particularly in the fall when the changing color of the leaves and dropping temperatures add to the magic. Spires of sandstone spring from the earth and point skyward; lush pine forests crawl up and slowly dissipate into mountain slopes, giving way to white peaks; endless plains of sand and saguaro undulate under a sun, that when the summer ends, sheds a gentle warmth rather than an anvil-like heat.

There are hundreds of ways to experience Arizona's natural beauty, but one of the simplest ways involves the very symbol of our human presence—asphalt highways. With thousands of miles of roadway to tool around on, you can easily see much of Arizona's spectacular scenery from the front seat of your car. And while you're driving, don't forget to search out the all-American roadside attractions, guaranteed to make travelers pull over and take notice of some strange amusement such as "the world's largest Kokopelli." Between the natural grandeur and the inspired silliness, just a few days of driving on Arizona's highways should make for a memorable trip.

There are a number of popular routes throughout the state. The Coronado Trail Scenic Byway is an amazing drive that takes you along the edge of the Apache-Sitgreaves National Forest, a two million acre preserve known for its cool camping (both modern and backwoods) and fantastic fishing. The Trail runs for 120 miles between Springerville and Clifton, rises in elevation from grasslands at 7000 feet to the evergreens at 8000 feet, and then drops dramatically as the route continues south, descending from the Mogollon Rim into the desert below. It's a fairly slow route (over four hours to cover 100 miles),

Courtesy of Greater Phoenix Convention and Visitors Bureau

but the spectacular views and changes of scenery make it well worth the turtle's pace. Besides, what are you in a hurry for? You're on vacation!

The route's history is also worth noting. Over 450 years ago, Francisco Vasquez de Coronado set out in search of the Seven Golden Cities of Cibola. What Coronado found when he arrived at Cibola was not a golden city, but a Zuni Indian pueblo. The find was

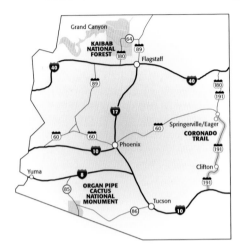

a bonanza from an archaeological point of view, but old Francisco wasn't too interested. In any case, U.S. Route 666/191, the highway that makes up the Coronado Trail, runs close to Coronado's path of disappointment. This fact, along with the strange and somewhat disturbing idea of driving on Route 666, will make this a drive to remember.

The beginning of fall is the ideal time for this drive. You'll be greeted by spectacular groves of aspens and oaks as they change from green to yellow and orange, plus the temperature will be comfortably brisk. If you do decide to come out in the summer though, the wildflower bloom brought on by monsoon season will make your trip just as colorful.

For a different landscape and a more adventurous experience, head down towards Mexico to the Organ Pipe Cactus National Monument. It lies on the Arizona-Mexico border and provides a perfect example of the Sonoran desert habitat. Puerto Blanco is the road to take here; it is one of Arizona's most beautiful byways, traveling deep into unspoiled backcountry. This road runs past a number of old mines and historical landmarks, including the Quitobaquito Oasis, a true desert oasis lined with trees and complete with a spring and a small pond. The water is home to an endangered species of desert pupfish, as well as coots, killdeer, and other varieties of desert birds. These sights alone, which are true rarities in the desert, are well worth the drive down.

If you've got a 4WD vehicle, you'll want to explore some of the unmarked, unmaintained roads that branch off Puerto Blanco deeper into the wilderness. On these, you'll find remnants of human habitation such as old ranch houses, more mines, and various other structures that will make you wonder how anyone could have lived in such a punishing environment. With that in mind, make sure you are well prepared; bring plenty of water and food, and make sure your car or truck is well maintained and fully fueled. There's very little in the way of services when you're off the beaten path.

At the south end of Puerto Blanco, you'll find yourself at Senita Basin, where you'll see the Monument's three major species of cactus—saguaro, organ pipe, and senita—all growing together. The Organ Pipe Monument is named after the cactus bearing the name, as this is one of the only places in Arizona where you will find this rare plant. Wildlife of all kinds surround you, so when you get out of the car, be sure to bring a camera to capture any bighorn sheep, coyotes, or javelinas that might cross your path.

If the desert is not necessarily your cup of tea, you might be more comfortable taking a nice autumn drive through the Kaibab National Forest by Williams and Flagstaff. No matter what your route, the trip will likely take all day, so be sure and pack a good lunch. It is likely that you'll do a lot of stopping for pictures of the fantastic mountain vistas.

There are a number of routes through the forest, so call the park office ahead of time

Photograph by Ray Bangs

WORLD'S LARGEST
KOKOPELLI

to get a detailed map. Some routes, like the Spring Valley Road, are gravel roads suitable for all cars. Others, such as the Perkinsville Road, are sometimes accessible, but are often restricted during bad weather to high clearance, 4WD vehicles. Before your trip, make sure to contact the District Office in Fredonia or the Kaibab park office for the latest access and weather information.

Each drive through the Kaibab National Forest provides great views of the natural wonders there: Kendrick Mountain, towering over the forest at 10,400 feet; Government Prairie, a large and seemingly misplaced grassland in the middle of the woods; and Coleman Lake, a great birding spot and popular waterfowl nesting area. Often, because some of the routes are fairly short, you will be able to do two or three in one day, giving yourself an opportunity to completely relax and take in the pristine wilderness.

Each of these drives will take you to a different part of the state and put you in a starkly different environment. Keep in mind that these are far from the only scenic drives Arizona has to offer; the Grand Canyon area alone boasts a large network of picturesque highways to explore. These three suggestions, however, are less heavily traveled because they are not as well known. Revel in the solitude and feeling of discovery—and take a journey.

Directions

Coronado Trail: Go Northeast from Phoenix on US-60 to US-180. Go South on US-180 to Eagar, a good starting point. Or, take I-10 East from Tucson to US-191, and turn north. Organ Pipe National Monument: From the north, follow AZ-85 through Ajo and Why. The Monument is 22 miles south of Why. From the east, take AZ-86 to Why, then turn south on AZ-85. Kaibab National Forest: The forest surrounds the Grand Canyon and extends to Flagstaff. Call the Kaibab National Forest for exact locations of routes and attractions.

For More Information

Coronado Trail, Forest Supervisor's Office, Springerville, AZ, 800/863-0546
    www.fs.fed.us/r3/asnf/resources/general.htm
Kaibab National Forest, Williams, AZ, 800/863-0546, www.fs.fed.us/r3/kai
Organ Pipe National Monument, Ajo, AZ, 520/387-6849, www.nps.gov/orpi

Recommended Reading

Green, Stewart & Johnson, Randy. *Arizona Scenic Drives.*
    Helena, MT: Falcon Publishing, 1996.
Hanson, Jonathan & Hanson, Roseann B. *Arizona and New Mexico: National Park Tours.*
    Tucson, AZ: Southwest Parks & Monuments Association, 1999.
Miller, Mark, et al. *Southwest: Utah, Arizona, and New Mexico (National Geographic's Driving Guides to America).* New York, NY: National Geographic Society, 1997.

Sedona Hot Air Ballooning

Floating Over Paradise

Red Rock country is one of the "don't miss" natural wonders of Arizona. Any picture you may have in your head of Southwestern beauty usually involves the majestic formations and dazzling colors that look almost too perfect in the area surrounding Sedona. Simply driving into town will afford you a healthy dose of the natural splendor, but the best way to see Sedona is from the morning sky in a hot air balloon. It's an adventure for both old and young, and a chance to experience the beauty of Arizona in a new way.

On September 19, 1783, a sheep, a duck, and a chicken became the first hot air ballooning adventurers. Since then, millions of people have taken the ride, jumping into wicker baskets and soaring miles above the ground in these brightly-colored, sometimes peculiarly-shaped crafts. This adventure is alive and well in Arizona, and in many ways the state is a perfect home for hot air ballooners. There is little dangerous wind or precipitation to speak of, and there are also plenty of open spaces for landing and taking off, an important fact given the sheer size of the balloons (otherwise known as envelopes). In a place like Sedona, hot air ballooning is a relaxing activity that gives participants time to look around and take in the amazing sights, as well as the space to begin and end the adventures safely.

Hot air ballooning has not changed much with the advent of new technology and materials. The object is to heat the massive pocket of air in the balloon to over one hundred degrees, at which point the balloon becomes lighter than the outside air and begins to rise. Good old air, heated by propane burners, is the only force of locomotion the pilot controls. Otherwise, the balloon floats on the air currents that surround it, moving as the air moves.

Photograph by Larry Lindahl

Courtesy of Red Rock Balloon Adventures

Red Rock Balloon Adventures is an outfit with over nine years of experience flying in the Red Rocks area. It has a perfect flying record and a staff of well-trained, FAA-certified pilots, who provide a nice background on both the history of ballooning and the Sedona area. Red Rock flies year-round, weather permitting. We suggest heading up in the fall or late spring, when the morning is going to be the most temperate. Their trips start at sunrise and usually last three to four hours, so there's still plenty of time to shop in Sedona or hike some of the terrain you've just soared over. After seeing everything from a few thousand feet up, we're betting you'll probably want to explore at least a little bit.

Your trip will start early, because flying conditions are optimal during the dawn. But the best thing about being out at that hour is the sunrise. The Sedona sun explodes over Red Rock country in dazzling reds, oranges, and yellows; it's a sight you've got to see for yourself. No photograph, however spectacular, can do the real thing justice. Do yourself a favor anyway and pack your camera ahead of time. At least your friends will have some idea of the beauty you were a part of.

Before lifting off, you will climb into the basket as the envelope is being filled with air. As the balloon "stands up," so will the basket with you in it. You will see the chase crew running around, pulling and pushing the balloon into position, and holding the ropes that keep you moored to the earth until the right moment. Then, as you feel the basket inch off the ground as the burners keep firing hot air into the envelope, the crew will let go of the ropes, and you'll start to rise faster. Before long, the chase crew will be a cluster of ants, and the natural scenery will make you forget that people even exist.

Sedona's red rocks exist in a state of primal suspended animation. The world they represent is not the one of highways and gift shops; they are from another era, and flying over them when the burners are silent will bring you to that place. Wildlife sightings are fairly frequent as well. We had a pretty light animal day, but we still saw three javelinas (wild pigs native to Arizona) and a herd of deer. Again, you might be kicking yourself if you don't catch these moments on film, so pack that camera the night before.

The scenery and fauna are not all there is to the balloon ride. The experience itself is worth the price of admission. Don't let the height scare you. The gondolas are very safe and secure, much bigger than they look from the ground. You won't feel like you're hanging on by a thread in a little basket once you're up and away. If there's anything objectionable about ballooning, it's the heat from the burners that supply the balloon's hot air. It's a bit uncomfortable at first, but if you wear a loose-fitting hat, it shouldn't bother you. Besides, the burner is most active when the balloon is rising; once you're up, the blasts come less often.

Most of us have only seen hot air balloons from a great distance and have no idea of how impressive they really are. They tower above the ground, and once you're in the air, take the time (between burner blasts) to look up into the mouth of the balloon. That's almost 100,000 cubic feet of hot air, all of it required to keep the gondola floating.

Once you are aloft, your balloon will float along silently, and you'll have a great chance to take in the sunrise. You'll coast along at an altitude ranging from one to two

thousand feet. If you're lucky, your pilot will be able to take you up much higher to the one-mile mark. Suffice it to say, at over five thousand feet above the ground, a mile is pretty high; enjoy the view and do your best to lean over and look down. It's a rush—just remember to take your hat off before you do it!

After your ride, the kind folks at Red Rock Balloon Adventures will have a pleasant finale in store for you—the fantastic First Flight Ceremony! You'll be treated to a champagne picnic and regaled with stories from your pilot about the history of ballooning and the trials of competitive balloon racing. It's interesting stuff. Our pilot also taught us the Ballooner's Prayer (people in big balloons a mile off the ground say a lot of prayers, apparently) and was an expert on the desert landscape around us. In all, a picnic is a perfect wind-down after the exhilarating ride and view.

Sedona is a highly spiritual and serene place. As the first rays peek over the eastern rocks, you too will see why so many people find rest and inspiration in the desert landscape. It is indeed a mystical experience, and one you will never forget.

Directions
Sedona is located just over 100 miles north of Phoenix. Follow I-17 north to exit 298. Signs clearly mark the turn on Highway 179 towards Sedona. Depending on weather, locations of departure may vary. Call and make a reservation, and then get directions over the phone or arrange to be picked up from a local hotel or resort. (The price includes a free video as well as the champagne brunch.)

Outfitters
Northern Light Balloon Expeditions, Sedona, AZ, 800/230-6222
    www.sedona.net/fun/balloon
Red Rock Balloon Adventures, Sedona, AZ, 800/258-3754, www.redrockballoons.com

Recommended Reading
Cheek, Lawrence W. *Sedona Calling: A Guide to Red Rock Country.*
    Phoenix, AZ: Arizona Highways, 1999.
Henkle, Teresa & Krause, Steve. *Sedona Guide: Day Hiking and Sightseeing*
    Arizona's Red Rock Country. Tempe, AZ: Pinyon Publishing, 1991.
Kalakuka, Christine & Stockwell, Brent. *Hot Air Balloons.*
    New York, NY: Metro Books, 1998.

Grand Canyon Railway

A Journey Through Time

If there is any mode of transportation that defines the West, it is the locomotive. A hundred years ago, railroad tracks criss-crossed the whole expanse of Arizona, delivering people to and from the boomtowns scattered around the territory. At that time, train travel was a relatively popular upper-class pursuit. But with the growing passion of driving the open road, passenger trains became a thing of the past, a relic of another era in America's adventurous history. Fortunately for those of you who missed this historic form of transportation, you can relive those days of genteel travel aboard one of Arizona's most cherished sources of mass transit: the Grand Canyon Railway. This fun little excursion combines a trip to the Canyon with a sample of rail travel, all for a reasonable price.

The train ride itself is the best reason to go on this adventure, but the convenience of seeing the Canyon this way is worth mentioning, too. First and foremost, you don't have to fight traffic into and out of the park; weekends in the fall can get pretty busy up there, and the volume of people can make the park's roads a bit frustrating. With the Railway, you simply ride the train from Williams into the Grand Canyon Depot, and then take in the amazing views and the sights of the Canyon's historical district. When you're due to return, reboard the train and enjoy a leisurely ride back to Williams where you can spend the night after your trip. It is an unhurried way to experience Arizona's greatest attraction, one that won't erase your pleasant memories, which can often happen during the long and sometimes frustrating drive out of the park.

Your big decision in regard to the train is what class of service you want to ride in. Coach is the cheapest and easiest class to ride in to and from the Canyon. Club and Main classes offer more amenities, such as breakfast and an alcohol beverage service, while the Dome class gives you an additional treat—a breathtaking view of the scenery from an upper-level enclosed glass dome. Finally, the Chief class provides an open-air platform,

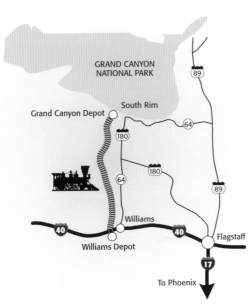

ideal for taking pictures and enjoying the temperate autumn air, all with a high level of comfort provided by the Railway's excellent staff. This class is the way to go for adults looking for a good pampering.

All along your trip with the Grand Canyon Railway, the spirit of the West will ride with you. To get started, visit the free Williams Depot museum, and then step outside and watch a dramatic Old West gunfight. Once you board the train, historic characters and Western musicians will take you back to another era and regale you with tales of travel in the nineteenth century. Ask questions and play along, especially if you're traveling with the kids.

As you continue on your way, though, the focus will move away from the human world and into the natural one, simply because of the land that surrounds your route. For sixty-five miles, the mountains and forests will open up before you, and you'll feel transported back in time by the land as well as the actors. The ride is meandering, so there's plenty of time for pictures. Be sure to tailor your selection in class to how good you want your view to be; if you want to take a ton of photos with your new wide-angle lens, don't settle for coach.

The most economical (and fun) way to ride the Grand Canyon Express is to make a weekend of it and purchase one of the package deals the railway offers in cooperation with the Grand Canyon National Park and the Fray Marcos Hotel in Williams. These packages run the gamut from the Family Getaway, geared towards providing two adults and two children with an overnight adventure for a minimal price (approximately $100 per person for the weekend), to the Canyon Railway Express, a package that provides an overnight stay in the Canyon as well as a guided motorcoach rim tour ($160-$260 per adult, depending on the season). With these combination packages, you get more bang for your buck, as well as a nice taste of what the Canyon has to offer. Chances are that after this first taste, you'll want to go back and spend a little more time there. Consider your rail trip a teaser for the mule ride or the hiking trip you'll take in the future.

In all, the Railway is a perfect introduction to the wonders of the Grand Canyon and northern Arizona's stunning landscape. It is also a step back into the past, to a time when porters carried your bags, the landscape rolled past you instead of under you, and half the pleasure of taking a trip was in the getting there. Like so many of the adventures in

Courtesy of Grand Canyon Railway

Courtesy of Grand Canyon Railway

this book, though, the main thing you'll take away from your weekend is the awe at how much Arizona has to offer. On this escape, you'll get to partake in the wild beauty and scenery of a true natural treasure, as well as the charm and history of the Old West. The Grand Canyon Railway has ample supplies of both.

Directions

From Flagstaff take I-40 west towards Williams for 32 miles to exit 163. Follow Grand Canyon Boulevard 1/2 mile south to the Grand Canyon Railway & Resort.

For More Information

Grand Canyon Railway, 800/843-8724, www.thetrain.com

Recommended Reading

Ambrose, Stephen. *Nothing Like It in the World: The Men Who Built the Transcontinental Railroad 1863-1869*. New York, NY: Simon & Schuster, 2000.

Gerber, Rudy J. *Grand Canyon Railroad Illustrated Guide Book*. Phoenix, AZ: Primer Publishing, 1990.

Gerber. Rudy J. *The Railroad and the Canyon*. Gretna, LA: Pelican Publishing Company, 1995.

Fishing and Camping
Old-Fashioned Fun For Everyone

Easy
$0–$100

When you were young, did you visit the local stream or fishing hole with your grandfather? Do you remember the first time you and your friends had a camping getaway without the folks? Maybe the trip you remember best is the first one with your kids—the "Daddy, what does mud taste like?" trip, or it could have been that romantic weekend your husband took you on. Maybe you've never even been camping! Whatever your prior experiences include, the first camping trip many of us ever take, the one that introduces us to the outdoors—to the campfire, the tents, and the elements—is the good old-fashioned fishing trip. The kind you can take in the White Mountains, Arizona's answer to the Great Lakes.

In early fall, much of Arizona is still struggling under the grip of summertime heat. The first direction most people head for escape is, naturally, up I-17 to Flagstaff. Unfortunately, if you go that way, you're risking a long wait in traffic. The Grand Canyon tourist season makes getting around up north a bit tough during the week, and especially rough on weekends. All the driving leaves little time for fun and frolicking. Fall is a good time to seek out Arizona's lesser-known destinations and take advantage of the special beauty offered to those who are willing to stray off the beaten path.

The White Mountains are far away from the extremes of both heat and humanity. With the wide expanse of wilderness, it is not a crowded, high-volume tourist destination, and the higher elevations (2,500-10,000 feet) drop the temperatures into an acceptable range. The area is steeped in Native American culture, as three reservations surround the small towns like Pinetop, Show Low, and Snowflake that dot the mountains. These hamlets are great places to stock up on supplies before heading out on your adventure.

This trip is not meant to be a three-day hike into the trackless wild. It is a relaxing jaunt into the White Mountains in pursuit of two things: rest and relaxation. The fish nibbling on your hook is just a bonus! As such, you'll want to pick campsites that are not only close to the waterborne action, but provide all the amenities a campsite can, e.g., drinking water, restrooms, showers, firewood, etc. There is no better way to get access to all of the qualities you're looking for than to find a clean, out-of-the-way campground and disappear for a while. If you are looking to rough it a little more, lucky for you, the White Mountains are full of these kind of places too, and nearly every one is within spitting distance of some of Arizona's finest fishing lakes.

You can get information about any of the campgrounds through the White Mountains Online website, one of the most well organized tourism sites in the state. The campgrounds are scattered across the White Mountain Apache Reservation and the Apache-Sitgreaves National Forest, and offer varying amenities and prices. Some are more oriented towards RVs, offering berths with full hookups. Others are only managed part of the year, if at all, and they offer water, access to fishing, and a few flat spots where you can pitch a tent.

The campground information at White Mountains Online is extensive and specific; if you go there first, you most likely won't be stuck with any surprises when you pull up to your campsite. Another important resource is the fantastic fishing report put together by the Arizona Game and Fish Department, which gives you tons of information about fishing around the state. Because fishing conditions change day to day throughout the

Photograph by Klaus Kranz

year depending on recent stocking, weather, and a host of other factors, make sure you check with the hotline before heading out.

If you want to take some more of the guesswork out of picking your lake, hire a guide and leave the fish finding to them. There are several guide services in the White Mountain area, many of which leave from Phoenix and will organize the whole trip for you. They can do everything from teaching you to fly fish to taking your family to the hotspots where your kids are most likely to pull newly stocked trout out of the water. Each guide service offers a variety of programs, from half-day lessons to overnight stays with lodging included. It's also a good way to go if you don't know a crappie from a carp.

Keep in mind that many of the campgrounds mentioned, along with the waters near them, are located on Native American land; as such, you will need to get permits for camping and fishing from the reservation. Once you pick a general area, call the phone numbers provided for more permit information. They are inexpensive, easy enough to obtain, and the best part is that you are normally not required to have an Arizona fishing license if you are not a frequent angler. With a variety of permits available, you'll have plenty of camping and fishing options.

We must not forget about the fish, especially since that's the bonus you're seeking in the White Mountains. There are so many varieties worth catching here that your head will spin. Trout are the biggest draws, as five species swim in White Mountain lakes. You can hit just about any lake and find trout of some type, as they are the most stocked fish in the area. Brook, cutthroat, and rainbow trout are all stocked in White Mountain waters, and brown trout, a species imported from Europe in 1931, reproduce naturally. The fifth species, the Apache trout, requires a little instruction. Besides being Arizona's state fish, it is a threatened species, which means you can't catch it and keep it. With these endangered fish, you must follow the strict catch and release policy.

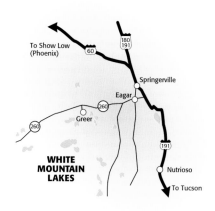

If you're wondering what you'll be able to catch and fry up for dinner, be assured that there are many other interesting fish in the White Mountain lakes. If you are on Ackre Lake or Lee Valley Lake, you might happen to hook an Arctic grayling, one of the more exotic species. Walleye lurk the waters of the Lyman Reservoir, and the McNary Millponds give you sixty fishable acres of pike and yellow bullhead. Channel cats are just about everywhere. So, when you look at the big picture, you shouldn't have any shortage of fish to catch. Make sure you get that fishing bulletin before you set out, and you'll be a happy angler.

And that's what it's all about—enjoying the fresh air, sleeping out in nature, and pulling fish out of the water. Whether you set them free or take them to camp for dinner, your purpose in these woods will have been fulfilled. After your R & R in the White Mountains, you will truly feel that all is right with the world.

Directions

To get to the general vicinity of the White Mountains, take US-60 east out of Phoenix. That will get you to Show Low; from there Greer, Pinetop, and the rest of the White Mountain towns are close by. From Tucson, take Route 10 east until you hit US-191. That will take you up and into the White Mountain wilderness. Call the U.S. Forest Service for more specific campground directions.

Outfitters

Anglers and Hunters Travel (see coupon pg 209), Phoenix, AZ, 800/658-5740
     www.anhtrvl.com
Paradise Creek Anglers, Pinetop, AZ, 800/231-3831
     www.paradisecreekanglers.com
Troutback Flyfishing (see coupon pg 211), Show Low, AZ, 800/903-4092
     www.troutback.com

For More Information

Apache-Sitgreaves National Forest, Springerville, AZ, 520/333-4301, www.fs.fed.us/r3/asnf
Arizona Game & Fish Dept., 602/942-3000, www.gf.state.az.us
White Mountain Apache Fish & Game Dept., White River, AZ, 520/338-4385
White Mountains Online, www.wmonline.com

Recommended Reading

Hirsch, Bob. *Outdoors in Arizona: A Guide to Fishing and Hunting.*
     Phoenix, AZ: Arizona Highways, 1988.
Meck, Charles R. & Rohmer, John. *Arizona Trout Streams and Their*
     Hatches: Fly-Fishing in the High Deserts of Arizona and Western New Mexico.
     Woodstock, VT: Backcountry Publications, 1998.
Sagi, Guy J. *Fishing Arizona: The Guide to Arizona's Best Fishing!*
     Phoenix, AZ: Golden West Publishing, 1998.

31 Experience Bisbee

Mines and Museums

Easy
$0-$100

Throughout the United States, there are small towns that, by way of some mystic cosmic alignment, become centers of art and culture. Somehow, the quaint town atmosphere leads to rumors among educated, well-heeled, artsy folks that such-and-such a place is simply the place to be. New Hope, Pennsylvania; Boulder, Colorado; and Madison, Wisconsin are three examples of these chichi villages. But let's not forget little Bisbee, right here in Arizona.

Don't get the impression that this jewel is simply a pretty little town filled with antique stores and art colonies, though. History is just as much a part of its everyday life as the arts or leisure activities, perhaps even more so than in other communities. You can't help but notice that the Victorian architecture, prevalent in many of the older buildings, shows a past, as does the continued presence of the once prosperous mines. Perhaps this historical lore combined with the beauty and location of Bisbee is what brought the artists and antique dealers here in the first place.

Bisbee owes its existence and good fortune to electricity, or rather, to the conductivity of copper, and the huge copper deposits that were discovered in the countryside around the town. Located in the southeast corner of the state, close to Mexico, Bisbee has a 120-year history of mining that mirrors the story of copper mining in the West. By the late 1880s, Bisbee was already a major copper mining center, and the biggest city between St. Louis and California. It was, even then, an oasis of culture in the trackless wilderness of the West. Over the years, miners carved over 2000 miles of tunnel under rocky ground, searching for the metal that would change the way people around the world powered

Courtesy of Bisbee Chamber of Commerce

Courtesy of Bisbee Chamber of Commerce

their lives. And, if you're still wondering what's so great and interesting about copper, just turn off the lights, the running water, and every other appliance in your house, and see just how long you last. If not for Bisbee and the other copper towns webbed across the West, Edison's light bulb would have been just an interesting little trinket. The citizens of Bisbee remember the sacrifices their forefathers made in pursuit of the Electric Age, and they are very glad to share their heritage with everyone who pops through town.

When you first arrive, take some time to just stroll around, check out the architecture, and take in the general grandness of the community; Bisbee had rivers of cash flowing through it during the golden age of the mines, and it shows all around you. You can see proof of this when you look up at the magnificent old houses perched atop impossible ledges and cliffs, cut by hand from the rock. Another good way to get a feel for historical Bisbee is to check out a real mine. Queen Mine Tours offers a great tour down inside one of Arizona's oldest mines. An added treat is the fact that ex-miners lead the tours, and they paint an interesting picture of just what it meant to work down there, including a description of the real working conditions and the daily dangers they faced. All of them are well versed in the history and culture of the mines, so ask lots of questions and satisfy your curiosity.

The real centerpiece of Bisbee's mining memorial is the Bisbee Mining and Historical Museum. The museum tells the story of the Bisbee mines and the men who worked there, as well as the community life that grew up around them. So after you've seen the mine and the town, head over to the Museum and get the rest of the story. Through pictures and written accounts, the museum aptly depicts the growth of Bisbee in conjunction with the blooming of a new, electrically-powered world. In the spring of 2002, the Museum, with cooperation from the

Courtesy of Bisbee Chamber of Commerce

Smithsonian Institute, hopes to open its newest attraction: "Digging In: Bisbee's Mineral Heritage." This exhibit will chronicle even further the impact Bisbee's number one industry had on the world.

When you are finished perusing the history of Bisbee, you might want to take a little time to enjoy its present. On any given night, you can choose to dine in a variety of great restaurants and follow it with a night of dancing to live music. And being so steeped in the arts, Bisbee also offers poetry readings, theater, art shows, and other cultural activities; just check with the city Chamber of Commerce to see what's going on while you're there. It is this additional slew of activities, things to do when you're not learning about the city's history, that make Bisbee a great weekend trip. While most of Arizona's historical destinations celebrate wild outlaws and gunfights, Bisbee celebrates something much more important—the transition of the world and Arizona's part in it. Don't miss the story.

Directions

To get to the Museum, take I-10 east from Tucson and turn south on Hwy 80 at Benson. Follow 80 through Tombstone and keep heading south. Once you pass the junction with State Hwy 90 from Sierra Vista, you will begin to climb the Mule Mountains. At the top of the climb, you will pass through the tunnel just below Mule Pass; once through the tunnel, Bisbee is right in front of you. About a mile from the tunnel, take the main exit to Old Bisbee. Follow the exit road and you'll be on Main Street. The Museum is just ahead on the right.

For More Information

The Bisbee Chamber of Commerce, 866/224-7233, www.bisbeearizona.com
Bisbee Mining and Historical Museum, 520/432-7071
    www.bisbeemuseum.org
Queen Mine Tours, 118 Arizona Street, Bisbee, AZ, 520/432-2071
    www.amdest.com/az/Bisbee/QueenMine.html

Recommended Reading

Bush, Neil L. *Bisbee, Arizona Yesterday & Today: A Comparative View of the Queen of the Copper Camps.* Bisbee, AZ: Bisbee Image, 1992.
Hyde, Charles K. *Copper for America: The United States Copper Industry from Colonial Times to the 1990s.* Tucson, AZ: University of Arizona Press, 1998.
Shelton, Richard. *Going Back to Bisbee.* Tucson, AZ: University of Arizona Press, 1992.

Dude Ranch

Saddle Up, Cityslicker!

Medium
$100-$500+

After checking out an event like the World's Oldest Continuous Rodeo, or taking in the sights at Tombstone and the Old Tucson Movie Studios, you might feel a small twinge of disappointment, as if the Old West's history has passed you by. You say to yourself, "I could have ridden the range, driven 1,500 head of cattle 200 miles, and roped a runaway calf! If I'd only been born a century and a half earlier, I'd have shown 'em!" Well, put your money where your mouth is pilgrim. Saddle up at an Arizona dude ranch and prove you're not the city dandy everybody takes you for.

The Arizona Dude Ranch Association has over fifteen members, scattered all around the state. You'll find guest ranches that cater to just about any group of vacationers, as well as single adventurers looking for an authentic Old West experience. These ranches are located across Arizona's vast stretches of undeveloped land, especially in the less populated landscapes outside of Tucson.

Be prepared to spend a little money on this adventure, as the nightly rates at a dude ranch can run fairly high. The upside to these prices is that they will include a lot more than at your average resort. All three meals (home cooked by your hosts at most places) are usually included, as are the majority of your activities—riding, learning to brand, and even throwing a lasso. Be aware, though, that some ranches will charge extra for certain activities, so make sure you know what you're in for wallet-wise before you go. The best way to keep your costs down is to round up as many people as possible to take on the adventure; it is common for the daily rates to drop significantly with each additional person.

When looking for the perfect ranch, don't stop after one or two phone calls. There are ranches to suit all different styles, from the authentic, working ranch that allows you

Courtesy of Rancho de Los Caballeros

Courtesy of Rancho de Los Caballeros

to drive your own herd of cattle, to the family-friendly ranch where kids can feed and care for their own colts. Some of them are western resorts, offering a variety of tourist-related amenities along with their ranch activities. Rancho De Los Caballeros in Wickenburg, for example, is probably the most resort-like of Arizona's ranches. It boasts a championship golf course and tennis courts on site, as well as nearby shopping in downtown Wickenburg. Other adventures such as nature hikes, hot air balloon rides, and desert jeep tours are just a few more of the non-horse related activities you can enjoy in the daytime. When night falls, the ranch's on-site saloon provides drinks, cowboy ballads, friendly card games, and other welcome forms of "city" entertainment. For its Western-style fun the ranch provides expert instruction in trap and skeet shooting, as well as daily rides through the beautiful Sonoran Desert. And, during holidays in the spring, guests at Los Caballeros have the opportunity to compete against guests at neighboring ranches in real rodeos. Talk about living out your Wild West dreams!

For those of you with children, it can be a little difficult to find a ranch that provides entertainment for your young ones. Many of them recommend a minimum age of twelve or thirteen, and few actively seek out the kiddie crowd. Sprucedale Ranch south of Alpine, however, is a happy exception as they cater to families by offering a wide array of kid's activities. They provide an on-site playground and numerous little kittens to play with. And for those adults hoping to tire the little ones out before the day is over, Sprucedale requires child participation in the down-home chores of cow milking and caring for the colts. Pop in here for a perfect getaway weekend with the whole family.

Another brand of ranch, which has been called one of the most unique and accessible ranches in Arizona, is the brand-new Stagecoach Trails Guest Ranch in Yucca. Owners Dan and Carrie Rynders offer a wide variety of special arrangements for people who might not otherwise be able to enjoy the ranch due to physical challenges, including an arena for supervised riding and alternative forms of backcountry transportation, namely ATVs and off-road go-karts. Because of this flexibility, Stagecoach Trails provides a special chance for everyone to enjoy our amazing state, regardless of physical ability level. If you are concerned about your ability level or have special needs, Stagecoach is well worth checking out.

Finally, for those of you looking for a more authentic, less tourist/family oriented adventure, call one of the many ranches that will be more than happy to cater specifically to you. Bellota Ranch, located outside of Tucson, is one of these ranches. They claim that

119

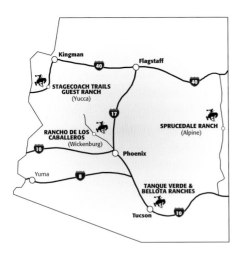

their preferred guests are cowpokes who already know their way around a horse. Founded in 1890, Bellota offers riders of at least intermediate skill a chance to participate in cattle drives, calf brandings, and roping lessons. The drives are not for the weak; typical days involve more than six hours in the saddle through some rough country, but it is a hardship well worth the memories and the incredible backcountry pictures you might capture on the way.

There are many more ranches in Arizona to choose from than just the ones mentioned here; these ranches are simply representative of the different kinds you'll find. Each one is a little different in what they offer, from size to accommodations to activities, and you should call around to a few of them before you make your selection. Keep in mind that each ranch caters to a certain customer, mostly because they are usually small, family-run operations that really work best with their preferred clientele. Just do your homework, and you'll have no trouble finding just the right ranch for your particular brand of needs.

Rides on the range, home-cooked meals, and more fun diversions than you can shake your spurs at—that is what Arizona's ranches are all about; so come out and experience the West first-hand. The next time you go to a rodeo you'll be able to say, "I could do that," and mean it.

Directions

When you book your reservations, the ranch you select will provide directions to their location.

Outfitters

Bellota Ranch, Tucson, AZ, 800/234-3833, www.bellota-ranch.com

Rancho De Los Caballeros (see coupon pg 211), Wickenburg, AZ 800/684-5030
www.ranchodeloscaballeros.com

Sprucedale Ranch, Alpine, AZ, 928/333-4984, www.sprucedaleranch.com

Stagecoach Trails Guest Ranch (see coupon pg 211), Yucca, AZ, 866/444-4471
www.stagecoachtrailsranch.com

Tanque Verde Guest Ranch, Tucson, AZ, 800/234-3833, www.tanqueverderanch.com

For More Information

The Arizona Dude Ranch Association, www.azdra.com

Recommended Reading

Erickson, John R. & Ward, Fay E. *The Cowboy at Work: All About His Job and How He Does It.* Norman, OK: University of Oklahoma Press, 1987.

Morris, Michele. *The Cowboy Life: A Saddlebag Guide for Dudes, Tenderfeet, and Cow Punchers Everywhere.* New York, NY: Fireside, 1993.

Starrs, Paul F. *Let the Cowboy Ride: Cattle Ranching in the American West (Creating the North American Landscape).* Baltimore, MD: John Hopkins University Press, 2000.

Paintball

Bang! Bang! You're Red!

Medium
$0–$100

Your camouflage fatigues are heavy after the sprint from your safe hole in the ground to the perimeter of the battle, this killing zone where two of your people have already had legs and arms blown off and been dragged off the field. The enemy is dug in hard behind four boulders that give them cover (and a view) on all sides, except for a tiny bit of obstructed space on their left flank. From your hole, you pinpoint their weakness and hope you might make it over the field without any of them seeing you.

The scout that found your hole didn't get the chance to communicate your position; you made sure of that when you put a slug in his chest. So you took the chance and bounded out, catching Reynolds from the corner of your eye—Reynolds, your friend, the guy you were buying a beer for last night out in the demilitarized zone. Now he was hit, red spraying up around his throat from the shot that took him in the shoulder. You curse softly as you hit the ground behind a tree; he was your cover. Looks like if you want

something done, you do it yourself. You swear that afterwards, Reynolds buys the beer. You'll make sure of that.

Paintball, Skirmish, Survival—whatever name this game goes by in your area, if you've never played before, you're missing one of the most unique, fun, and strangely rewarding adventures out there. Almost anyone can play, and whatever your feelings are about guns, the military, etc., this activity is not just for wannabe Green Berets. Paintball (the preferred term of those who play the game frequently) combines teamwork with individual cunning and strategy, along with a healthy dose of competition.

In its most basic form, paintball brings together two teams and pits them against each other in a modified game of Capture the Flag. The twist is in how one team "puts out" members of the other team; each player is equipped with a pneumatic air gun which fires biodegradable gelatin capsules of varying colors. These capsules break on impact, leaving a spray of water-based paint wherever you're hit. (Don't worry, moms, dads, and camouflaged fashionistas—the splats wash out easily.) Games are won when a

Courtesy of Command Post

player successfully returns the opponents' flag to his or her own headquarters.

Games last around 20 minutes, allowing 8-12 games to be played in about four hours. Prices range from $20-$40 per person, depending on the field and the day you're playing, plus another $5-$10 for rental equipment. The games do move quickly, though, so adrenaline starts pumping from the very first starting horn and flows until the end of the last game. Teams have varying numbers of people on them depending on who else is playing that day, or if there is a tournament going on. For a first timer playing on open weekends (the usual practice at paintball fields), figure on teams from ten to upwards of forty people.

If it is your first time, most paintball facilities will provide the rental equipment (guns, fatigues, paint, etc.) Bear in mind, though, that when you run out of ammo, you'll have to buy more. Play like a sniper, not Rambo. The one piece of gear you need to bring is footwear, so be sure to bring boots or sneakers that are comfortable, supportive, and that you don't mind having covered with dirt. And remember—white tennis shoes show up very nicely against a muddy brown background. (That's a bad thing, in case you're wondering.)

As one would expect from any sport in which tiny projectiles hurl through the air at high speeds, safety is an important concern for paintball aficionados. When you get shot, it does sting just a little (wear multiple light layers to minimize this), though you may not even feel it with all the action happening around you and the adrenaline moving through your veins. Your most important piece of equipment is your goggles; you may even want to consider buying a pair of no-fog eyewear before playing, as the exertion, flying paint, and outdoor debris can make vision a tricky proposition. The game is much more fun when you can see, as is life after the game; the rule "never take off your goggles" is as important to the paintballer as "don't eat the yellow snow" is to alpiners. Never, ever do it.

If your first paintball experience hooks you, then you should be aware that there are enough people in the same boat for there to be a bono fide paintball community, complete with professional tournaments, equipment reviews, magazines, and websites galore. Experience shows them to be a generally jovial group of people, passionate about their sport and happy to welcome new enthusiasts. If you crave paintball without the benefit of a group to play with, this community will patch you in with people who want to play as badly as you do. Any of the Arizona paintball sites you go to will be able to give you information on how to join the group, as well as sell you more high-end gear (semi-automatic paint guns, etc.). Some paintball guns cost well over $1,000, but the cost is worth it if you intend to play the game seriously.

Enjoying paintball is not the exclusive right of gun nuts or paramilitary phonies. It's a sport suitable for the whole family (though most sites require kids to be a little older, 12-14 and up), and a great way to experience Arizona's wilderness areas and ridiculously good weather. Playing indoors is fun, but outside, where you get the chance to roll around in the mud, diving over logs and under leaves, is infinitely better. And remember—the dirtier you get, the more likely your opponent is to mistake your filthy hide for a lump of ground.

Courtesy of Command Post

Let's not forget about the team sports factor. After a certain age, many of us lose the chance to play on any team outside of beer-league softball. We lose that comradery and thrill of competition. Paintball is a perfect activity for getting a little taste of it again; just round up a couple of your softball buddies and head out. Or, if you're on vacation, start a family team. But dads beware—friendly fire is a big concern, so don't upset the family before the big game. It is a good idea to let Junior stay at the hotel pool for an extra hour, and take the wife to that nice Mexican restaurant she keeps talking about. These friendly peace offerings could end up being the difference between life and a paint capsule to the spine.

Directions

There are numerous paintball facilities located throughout the state. Call the one closest to you for directions.

Outfitters

Battle Zone (see coupon pg 211), 1540 W. Hatcher Rd., Phoenix, AZ, 602/861-2255

Command Post (see coupon pg 211), 2111 S. Alma School Rd., Mesa, AZ
480/755-2442, www.azpaintball.com

Command Post (see coupon pg 211), 4139 W. Bell Rd., Phoenix, AZ
602/863-2569, www.azpaintball.com

Command Post (see coupon pg 211), 1432 N. Scottsdale Rd., Tempe, AZ
480/970-6329, www.azpaintball.com

Desert Fox Paintball, 9651 S. Houghton Rd., Tucson, AZ, 520/574-9232
www.desertfoxpaintball.com

Sportsmen's Center, Building 15423 Garden Canyon Rd., Sierra Vista, AZ
Ft. Hauchuca Military base, 520/533-7085

Recommended Reading

Barnes, Bill. *Paintball! Strategies and Tactics.* Memphis, TN: Mustang Publishing, 1993.

Elbe, Ronald E. *Paintball, the Wizard's Way: The Authoritative Book on Paintball Equipment, Strategy, and Tactics.* Southport, CT: Blacksmith Publishing Corporation, 1994.

Little, John R. *Ultimate Guide to Paintball.* New York, NY: McGraw Hill, 2001.

Astronomy and Stargazing

Sonora by Starlight

Medium
$0-$100

Light pollution prevents most city dwellers from taking in what the night sky really has to offer. Sure, there are stars up there, weak, dim points that we see when we get into the suburbs or drive outside of town, but often they do not impress us. They are a far cry from the skies that we remember from our childhood—crowded with swarming stars and streaks, chaotic with light and the simulated movement of twinkling points. For most of us, our lives have crowded out the stars and rendered them a less-than-magical nighttime backdrop.

The stars, though, are not legends to be forgotten when people no longer pay attention to them. They are still up there, burning as they have forever. If you can leave the lights of civilization behind, you will discover that in their uninterrupted glory, they still have the power to awe and inspire us. Luckily, Arizona's own Kitt Peak Observatory is located under some of the most star-friendly skies in the country, away from the light pollution of Tucson and Phoenix. Kitt Peak was the first national observatory in the country and

Courtesy of Greater Phoenix Convention and Visitors Bureau, Justin Associates, Inc.

Courtesy of Arizona Office of Tourism

today houses the world's largest collection of telescopes.

Think about it for a minute, and you'll realize that Arizona is the perfect location for a facility like Kitt Peak. The weather here is a natural fit; cloud cover is almost invariably sparse, and even the temperature during an autumn visit is comfortable compared to the biting cold fall weather you'd find at many northern stargazing destinations. The air is very dry too, perfect for sensitive electronic and optical equipment. And Kitt Peak is located in the mountains, on the Tohono O'odham Reservation near Tucson. Try to design a location for a multi-million dollar stargazing center, and you will have a hard time coming up with something better than this.

Kitt Peak offers a few different experiences for stargazing, but their most popular one is the nighttime observation program. The fun starts forty-five minutes before sundown when you arrive at the observatory and enjoy a light dinner. Then you'll stroll through the on-site museum and familiarize yourself with the facility, as well as learn some of astronomy's basic concepts and procedures. If you're a beginner, this is a good time to learn how the telescopes work and find out what astronomers are looking at besides the beauty of the stars. You more experienced star hounds will appreciate the history lesson as you learn about the specs on the observatory's array of equipment. The four-meter Mayall telescope, for example, is over eighteen stories tall and houses a fifteen-ton reflective mirror polished to one millionth of an inch. Its reflective aluminum coating is one-thousandth the thickness of a human hair. Amazing stuff.

Once the sun sets, the real fun begins. Everyone is equipped with a pair of binoculars at dusk so that you can scout the sky, searching for the heavenly features and constellations that you'll be focusing on later. One suggestion—Kitt Peak is located at 6800' in elevation, and since it's nighttime, dress accordingly. The temperatures can dip to freezing during winter and on some chilly fall nights. You'll be a happier observer if you can control your shivering long enough to focus your eyes.

After this initial observing, you and your group (make reservations ahead of time—spots fill up quickly) will make your way inside and use the eighteen-inch observatory telescope to get an up-close view of the stars and planets. This powerful tool will blow away any home telescope you may have been looking through; if you are a regular visitor in the night sky, you may find yourself vowing to return during your first turn at the

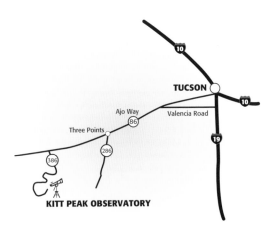

KITT PEAK OBSERVATORY

scope. But both experienced stargazers and first-timers alike will be amazed by the sky you'll see from Kitt Peak. The experience is enough to make you wish, for just a little while, that the city lights weren't so bright.

Your Kitt Peak adventure will last approximately four hours. The tours run seven nights a week during fall, winter, and spring, but the nightly observations are suspended from mid-July to August due to the monsoons and the clouds they bring. The time of year you go dictates to some extent what you'll see; constellations change during the year, and heavenly bodies like planets and galaxies are only visible at certain times. Contact the observatory to see what's going on in the interstellar neighborhood during your visit.

If one night under the stars isn't enough for you, you have a few options. If you're a native Arizonan with a telescope of your own or a visitor who totes one along, simply go out into the desert hinterlands and set up shop using what you learned at Kitt Peak in

addition to your own expertise. If you are a scopeless beginner looking for more experience, or simply find yourself stuck in one of our two most light-infected cities, check out one of Arizona's planetariums and get your fix.

Flandrau Science Center and Planetarium in Tucson and the Arizona Science Center in Phoenix both offer planetarium shows to the public. Planetarium shows don't quite put you out there with the stars themselves, but they do make for a fun experience nonetheless. Plus, they are very educational and often focus on specific aspects of our relationship with the heavens (exploring Mars, the sun, etc.) Above all, the shows are entertaining, and a great way to introduce kids and uninitiated adults to the cosmos. They are both parts of bigger museums, too, so along with your indoor stargazing you'll be able to wander through numerous other science exhibits.

Hopefully, experiences like these can help you again appreciate the twinkling wonders of childhood and cause you to start actively pursuing educational experiences like the museums or Kitt Peak observatory. Soon you'll know at least a little more than "Oh, that's the Big Dipper!"

Directions

To get to Kitt Peak Observatory from Tucson take I-10 to I-19 South. Less than 1 mile is Ajo Way (Hwy 86). Take this exit west (right). Proceed past Ryan Airfield and Three Points. Continue until the junction with 386, the Kitt Peak turnoff, and turn left onto 386. The Kitt Peak Visitor Center is located at the summit (12 miles).

For More Information

Arizona Science Center, 600 E. Washington St., Phoenix, AZ, 602/716-2000
    www.azscience.org
Flandrau Science Center and Planetarium, University Of Arizona, Tucson, AZ
    520/621-4515, www.flandrau.org
Kitt Peak Observatory (see coupon pg 211), 950 N. Cherry Ave., Tucson, AZ
    520/318-8200 (Recorded Info), 520/318-8726 (Visitor Center)
    www.noao.edu/kpno/kpno.html

Astronomy Clubs

East Valley Astronomy Club, www.eastvalleyastronomy.org
Phoenix Astronomical Society, http://pastimes.homestead.com/pastimes.html
Saguaro Astronomy Club, www.saguaroastro.org
Sun City West Astronomy Club, www.geocities.com/scwac

Recommended Reading

Bakich, Michael E. *The Cambridge Guide to the Constellations.*
    Cambridge, England: Cambridge University Press, 1995.
Chartrand, Mark R. *National Audubon Society Field Guide to the Night Sky.*
    New York, NY: Knopf, 1991.
Staal, Julius D. W. *The New Patterns in the Sky: Myths and Legends of the Stars.*
    Blacksburg, VA: McDonald & Woodward Publishing Company, 1996.

35 National Wildlife Refuges

Where the Wild Things Roam

Medium
$0-$100

So last weekend you decided to go camping in the White Mountains. Good choice. You caught six decent-sized trout (so you claim) and saw a herd of elk grazing in an open field. But what was that other pig-like creature you saw rooting though the weeds?

That piggish javelina you saw is actually fairly common, and since they often run in herds, you probably missed others hiding nearby in the brush. If it weren't for the zoo, many Arizonans would have no idea what a javelina looks like off the printed page. Fewer people still have ever seen a rattlesnake or a mountain lion in the wild, again both common if you escape into their world. For those of you who are interested in learning more about our native animals, Arizona offers two perfect places to put you in close contact with our furred, feathered, and finned friends: Havasu and Bill Williams National Wildlife Refuges. In comparison to zoos, which show off exotic animals in small confined areas, these Wildlife Refuges offer a little more excitement when you actually encounter the wild critters on their home turf.

Both the Havasu and Williams Refuges have been designated as non-development areas in order to protect the native plants and animals. Because the animals are living and breeding in their natural environments, your chances of exciting close encounters, rare species sightings, and terrific photo opportunities are very good. Of course, it should go

Courtesy of Lake Havasu Tourism Bureau

without saying, but there will always be some joker who wants to harass a rattlesnake, tease a bighorn, or wrestle a mountain lion. Do not be one of those people, because rest assured, you'll get what you deserve when that bighorn decides to defend his territory, that cougar bites back, or that rattlesnake isn't interested in playing with you. You're on their turf—respect that and respect them.

Arizona has long been a protector of its treasured native animal population. The Havasu Refuge was established in 1941, designated to protect a 24-mile stretch of the Colorado River that is home to a rare community of animals. Until 1993, the Bill Williams Refuge was a part of the Havasu Refuge. The following year, after the two areas had been separated, Havasu was declared one of America's few designated Wilderness Areas. With 37,515 acres of water and shoreline, Havasu provides an ecological cross-section with its large man-made marsh, expansive backwater areas, curved mountain peaks and cliffs, rock and gravel-strewn hills, and even sand dunes. This Refuge is divided

between Arizona and California, and the majority of the acreage falls on the east side of the Colorado River. The Williams Refuge, covering 6,055 acres all within Arizona, is home to one of the last native riparian (riverside) habitats in the lower Colorado River valley, making it a vital breeding ground and wintering area. Put the two Refuges together, and you'll be hard-pressed to find more geographical or zoological variety anywhere else in the country!

On any given day at either Refuge, you're liable to see waterbirds like egrets, kingfishers, and grebes, as well as rare desert reptiles, including the endangered desert tortoise and the legendary Gila monster, one of the world's only poisonous lizards. Rattlesnakes are more common in the warmer months.

The late fall and winter are the best times to be here for bird watching; there are hundreds of bird species that winter here or at least pass through on their way even farther south. American white pelicans and great blue herons are fairly common during the fall, and you even stand a chance of seeing a bald eagle or peregrine falcon. Obviously, with the multitude of wings in the air, it's a good idea to bring binoculars.

There are also mammals galore running around the Refuges, everything from bighorn sheep to bobcats, beavers, mountain lions, foxes, and javelinas. Both areas are simply crawling with animals, and though you may not see every species wandering the landscape, you'll more than likely see something. The abundance of life means that you'll have the opportunity for great photos to fill in your latest album or to show your kids just what the heck a javelina looks like. In any case, the animals are all around you just waiting to be noticed.

Besides wildlife viewing and photography, hunting and fishing are allowed during season on both Refuges. The Arizona Game and Fish Department has all the information to apply for the variety of permits you might need. If you choose to hunt or fish, remember that you are on a Refuge, and that you must follow all of the rules and regulations.

Courtesy of Lake Havasu Tourism Bureau

In the summertime, the heat is definitely a concern. Bring plenty of water and a big hat if you test the scorching sun; temperatures of 115 degrees and higher are not uncommon between June and September. If you decide to brave the heat, remember that the animals are concerned with keeping cool as well, and they might not be prancing around like runway models to get their photos taken. Wait until the temperatures drop and the birds stop by for the winter, then head over.

Access to both Refuges is free, which is perfect for families and those of us trying to stretch our adventure dollars to the limit. There will be a fee for any additional activities such as boating, hunting, or fishing. Camping is permitted on the Arizona-side shoreline, but no fires are allowed in the Wilderness. Hiking, biking, and auto touring are all free and plentiful, making the Refuges not only nice places to visit once, but also excellent destinations to seek out again and again.

Directions

The Havasu Refuge is located southeast of Needles, CA. To get to the entrance from Needles, take Harbor Avenue north, then turn right onto Mohave County 1 and follow the signs. The Williams Refuge is located approximately 17 miles north of Parker on Hwy 95. From Lake Havasu City, head south on 95. The office is across from the Havasu Pumping Plant on the west side of road, between mile marker 160 and 161.

For More Information

Bill Williams National Wildlife Refuge , 60911 Highway 95, Parker, AZ, 928/667-4144
Havasu National Wildlife Refuge , P.O. Box 3009, Needles, CA, 760/326-3853
Lake Havasu Tourism Bureau, 800/242-8278, www.golakehavasu.com

Recommended Reading

Carr, John. *Arizona Wildlife Viewing Guide.* Helena, MT: Falcon Press, 1992.
Lazaroff, David. *Arizona-Sonora Desert Museum Book of Answers.*
    Tucson, AZ: Arizona-Sonora Desert Museum Press, 1998.
Phillips, Steven. *A Natural History of the Sonoran Desert.*
    Berkeley, CA: University of California Press, 1999.

36 Soaring

Look Ma, No Engine!

**Medium
$0-$100**

The easiest, most economical, and most exciting sure-fire way to experience some serious Gs is to jump into the passenger seat of a glider about to depart for an aerobatics flight. It starts out calm enough with only a few bumps here and there, but just after you realize that you and the pilot have been released from the tow plane, you are suddenly in the middle of a stomach-churning maelstrom. Unless you are a diehard thrill-seeker, we highly advise that you opt for an introductory flight without any of the "extras" on your first time up. Flying through the air in what amounts to a plane without an engine will be excitement enough. And don't worry, Arizona's awesome air currents will provide plentiful heart-in-your-throat action.

Gliding, also known as soaring, is flying in a motorless sailplane using the naturally occurring atmospheric phenomena called lift. Arizona air is arguably the world's best, because all three forms of lift energy are present, often in the same general location and to varying degrees year round. Experienced pilots can circle tightly in these different lifts until high enough to fly "cross-country," or at least well beyond the launch site in search of more thermals. In Arizona, many pilots even enjoy mid-summer flights from Phoenix to the Grand Canyon (and back). The world record distance in a sailplane is almost 1250 miles. With more experience, all day flights are not uncommon.

Thermals, the first type of lift energy, are columns of warm, rising air, which with the famed Arizona sun, are widespread year round. The second type of energy is called ridge lift, where air currents following the land's terrain rise over the windward side of a hill and create a brief, upward surge. The third and often most exciting type is wave lift, present when very powerful winds deflect off a ridge or mountain and shoot forcefully upwards. Wave lift is intensified during the late summer monsoon season, and the incredibly turbulent air makes for the best expert-level soaring. Wave flights can reach altitudes up to almost 50,000 feet, but unfortunately, the legal limit is only 18,000 feet. A note to adrenaline junkies—these powerful sources of lift energy also provide the fuel for the brain-numbing aerobatic rides. Hitting a fierce wave of rising air can feel roughly the same as being slingshotted straight up. If you are a roller-coaster fanatic, then the aerobatics flight is definitely for you.

Getting your glider pilot license, however, is not a one-day or weekend affair, even for seasoned pilots seeking their glider rating. Just getting used to the quiet thrill of soaring takes some time. It can be oddly eerie when you are cruising off a thermal, knowing that your sailplane does not have an engine. You'll have a tendency to be extra careful, especially at first, but all pilots and passengers are required to wear a parachute just in case of any problems. Once you are licensed, though, the sport becomes quite addictive. Many Arizona pilots fly in the state competition series as well as regional, national, and even international events.

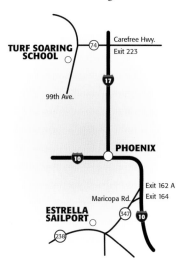

The first step is to take an introductory flight, reasonably priced at around $100 and perfect for introducing you to soaring. Two Phoenix-area commercial gliding operations, Arizona Soaring at Estrella Sailport and Turf Soaring School, stand out as the best and both offer first-timer flights with licensed instructor pilots. The introductory flights are available in several different sailplanes, starting with the most basic training gliders and going up to the highest performance racers. You will be towed up by a plane (with an engine!) and after being released, your instructor will explain and demonstrate the basic flying techniques. As you become more comfortable with the experience, you'll even get the opportunity to take over the controls and enjoy the wonder of free flight. Should you make a mistake, your instructor is right there with an identical set of controls, so don't worry about messing things up too much. Just don't try anything really crazy your first time up. That will come with time!

Courtesy of Turf Soaring School

Courtesy of Turf Soaring School

The length of the flight somewhat depends on the flying conditions, but introductory flights are just long enough for you to have a great time and leave you wanting more. The glass-encased cockpit is well suited for enjoying the scenery thousands of feet below. You will race across open desert, sometimes rising hundreds of feet in mere seconds with many of the powerful thermals. Prepare yourself if you see a mountain drawing closer. Winds whipping off these giants can rocket you upwards even more easily than hot air. Even though there is no engine, sailplanes are still incredibly agile and you can feel the G-forces whenever the pilot banks sharply. Taking a sailplane ride is the perfect way to spend a long afternoon, but just remember…it won't necessarily be a relaxing one. Soaring is a thrill!

Another option for that first flight is to experience gliding with your significant other. If your combined weight is less than 300 pounds, the two of you can enjoy a romantic mile-high ride together, possibly before a night out on the town. This would certainly be one delightful date and one neither of you would soon forget.

When you finally land, your pilot will enter the flight information in a logbook, which works well as a souvenir or as the first completed checkmark on your glider pilot training. Additional training flights can be booked to fit your schedule. If you're relaxed while flying during the lessons, take instructions well, and have the time, you could be certified to fly solo after only 20 to 30 flights.

Starting at around $10,000, sailplanes can be quite expensive, causing many potential pilots to hold off on pursuing soaring as a full-time hobby. The high-performance fiberglass or carbon fiber sailplanes are well beyond many people's budget, so one option is to gather several friends and purchase a glider as a group and share the airtime. A second option is to rent a sailplane from a commercial operation or one of the numerous clubs. Either way, gliding is much less expensive than flying airplanes, and to most, it is a lot more fun.

So the next time you are driving along a flat section of desert and you notice a "dust-devil," imagine flying through it. This is just one of the possibilities in a sailplane; soaring can be as mellow or as exciting as you make it. The gliders are high-performance machines that are very safe, well maintained, and inspected regularly. Since you will not be flying solo, this adventure is within everyone's skill level. The instructors and pilots at Arizona Soaring and Turf Soaring School are top-notch, and since most have logged thousands of hours in the air, you'll be in very accomplished, professional hands. The only difficult part will be to convince yourself that you really can fly.

Directions

To get to Estrella Sailport from Phoenix follow I-10 east towards Tucson. Exit at 162A or 164 and follow Maricopa Rd. (Hwy 347) for approximately 15 miles. Turn right (west) on Hwy 238. Drive 6.5 miles to Estrella Sailport. To get to the Turf Soaring School from Phoenix take I-17 north to the Carefree Highway exit. Turn left (west). Go left (south) on 99th Ave. Follow the signs.

Outfitters

Arizona Soaring (see coupon pg 213), Maricopa, AZ, 520/568-2318
    www.azsoaring.com
Turf Soaring School (see coupon pg 213), Peoria, AZ, 602/439-3621
    www.turfsoaring.com

For More Information

Arizona Soaring Association, www.asa-soaring.org
Tucson Soaring Club, www.tucsonsoaring.org

Recommended Reading

Piggot, Derek. *Understanding Gliding: The Principles of Soaring Flight.*
    London, England: A&C Black, 1998.
Thomas, Fred. *Fundamentals of Sailplane Design.*
    College Park, MD: College Park Press, 1999.

37 Hiking the Arizona Trail

Difficult
$0-$100

790 Miles, If You've Got the Time

Arizona is certainly well known for its spectacular hiking, as the magic of the desert draws millions of tourists annually. However, besides the saguaro-strewn desert, Arizona offers a variety of terrain and ecological zones. While it's hard to imagine hiking through the snowy San Francisco Mountains, the extensive ponderosa forests, and the sunny Sonoran Desert all on one continuous trail, it's possible, if you've got the time.

During a hike through the Santa Rita Mountains sometime in the 1970s, Flagstaff schoolteacher Dale Shewalter came up with an idea—to create a long-distance, continuous trail from Utah to the Mexican border, linking all of Arizona's unique landscapes and regions. Shewalter imagined that rather than limiting themselves to one specific region

Photograph by Mark Scheyli

at a time, hikers would benefit from an opportunity to experience the whole Arizona panorama on one long trail.

During the summer of 1985, Shewalter scouted the route for such a trail, walking from Nogales, located on the border with Mexico, to Utah, mapping all the way and visualizing a network of trails that would unite to form a coherent and continuous route. He estimated a 750-mile trek from one end of the state to the other, capable of supporting hikers as well as mountain bikers and cross-country skiers. In 1988, the dream became a reality when construction of the Trail began, and Shewalter became the first Arizona Trail Coordinator. That year, seven miles of the Kaibab Plateau Trail opened, becoming the first public access segment of the greater Arizona Trail. Since then, work has continued non-stop on the rest of it, making for the greatest teaming of manpower and nature in the state's history.

The Arizona Trail is the ongoing realization of a western version of the Appalachian Trail, a long-distance route that captures all the natural beauty and adventure the country has to offer. Though it is still not entirely complete, over 575 miles of trail have been designated and signed. The Trail is made up of preexisting routes incorporated into its length, as well as primitive roads (for linkage in areas without trails yet) and newly constructed stretches. When it is fully completed, the Trail will become one of the longest non-motorized routes in the country, and a premier destination for long-distance hikers.

You don't need to take on the whole thing to enjoy the Trail, though. There are trailheads scattered throughout the state, with plans for seventeen more in the works. Whether you're starting your trek in the northlands of Flagstaff or sampling the harsh landscape of the Sonoran desert, the Trail caters to all levels of skill, all desired trip

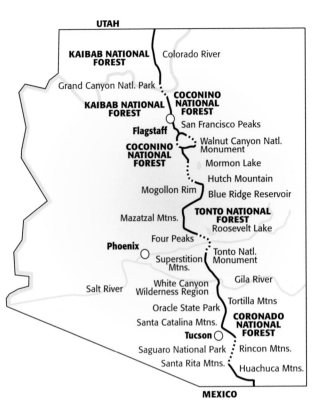

lengths, and all scenic interests. This is the epic Arizona adventure, a remarkable opportunity to experience the ecological diversity in a relatively short time. Since Arizona's mountain ranges are not linked, there's an ocean of variety. Pine trees give way to saguaro-spiked desert quickly and repeatedly. The diversity of plant and animal life is amazing too, and since the trail is largely backcountry, you're likely to see javelina, bighorn sheep, or hundreds of other species during your trek.

The Arizona Trail Association (ATA) is an organization dedicated to the continued building of the Trail, as well as its maintenance and public relations. For native Arizonans with an interest in the outdoors, membership in the ATA is a worthy pursuit, as the Trail is a valuable part of our continually growing outdoor heritage. For visitors, the ATA is a strong steward, providing hikers from around the world with an exciting and challenging destination. Volunteers from the ATA are responsible for building and maintaining the Trail, as well as planning and financing its future. It is a worthy organization, deserving of support and respect.

The best way to show respect, as well as reverence for the natural wonders the Trail has to offer, is to follow the "leave no trace" ethic espoused by the ATA. The ethic is merely a list of guidelines meant to keep the wilderness of the Arizona Trail as pristine as possible, so that future generations might benefit from it as much as we will. The rules are common sense—no littering, no straying from the trail into untouched wilderness areas, no waste in the water sources, and more—but together they make up a fundamental code of conduct for backcountry hiking that is well worth practicing. Another motivator is that most of the Trail is located on U.S. Forest Service land, so acting like a fool while you're on it might just get you arrested. Be careful, be smart, and respect the wilderness and your fellow hikers.

The Arizona Trail is not the toughest hike in the state, but it isn't a jaunt up the road either. Although accessible from a number of trailheads, long expanses of wilderness area, with no contact to the outside world, mean you should take the challenge seriously. Another little warning: despite the volunteer work force, a trail this long is hard to take care of, and as a result, portions are liable to be overgrown when you get to them. In other words, be sure to have some backcountry skills before setting out. Most of the trail segments are between twenty and forty miles long, perfect for a weekend trip, but tough on hikers who don't prepare properly. Get in shape with some day hiking and overnighters, and then take on whatever section of the Trail appeals to you the most. Contact

Photograph by John O'Neal

the ATA for more information about individual trail segments, as well as for information on permit and camping regulations.

There are no other trails in Arizona, and very few nationwide, that allow for the kind of long-distance, multiple landscape experience that the Arizona Trail provides. Hiking it in portions is the second-best way to experience everything the natural world of Arizona has to offer; the best is, of course, to take four months off when the trail is finished and hike the whole darn thing. It's a stretch, but keep dreaming. Who knows? By then, maybe that lottery habit will pay off.

Directions

The Arizona Trail has over forty trailheads scattered throughout the state. Simply contact the Arizona Trail Association to find out which ones are closest to you or to where you want to be. The map on their website is pretty general, but it gives a good idea of where the trail is, what it runs through, etc.

For More Information

The Arizona Trail Association, Phoenix, AZ, 602/252-4794, www.aztrail.org

Recommended Reading

Fayhee, John M. *Along the Arizona Trail.* Englewood, CO: Westcliffe Publishing, 1998.

Moran, Susan & Tighe, Kelly. *On the Arizona Trail: A Guide for Hikers, Cyclists, and Equestrians.* Boulder, CO: Pruett Publishing, 1998.

Townsend, Chris. *Crossing Arizona: A Solo Hike Through the Sky Islands and Deserts of the Arizona Trail.* Woodstock, VT: Countryman Press, 2002.

38 Learning to Rock Climb

Cams, Chalk, and Carabiners, Oh My!

Difficult
$0-$100

You can practice or prepare for many outdoor activities through exercise. Your skiing benefits from strong legs; hiking is easier and more fun with a strong set of lungs. Only rock climbers, however, can safely practice their art indoors, increasing their skill level in a perfect climate so they're ready when the elements present a bigger challenge.

Fortunately, beginners as well as experienced climbers can make use of this off-site preparation. What better way to learn a strenuous, rewarding sport like rock climbing than in the confines of a first-rate rock gym, complete with gear, instructors, and above all, a variety of walls for improving your technique. A great place to start is at the Phoenix Rock Gym. It provides the perfect starting point for beginners, as well as a great practice ground for seasoned climbers.

Climbing is a difficult sport. It makes use of all the body's muscles and every shred of the brain's focus and concentration. You can't approach it lightly, nor should you do so without the proper training. Some degree of physical fitness is required before even trying to climb; going straight from the couch to a sheer cliff face covered with two inch ledges for grips and steps is not a recipe for success. Before you even set foot in the rock gym, it's a good idea to get familiar with your closest exercise facility, or a home equivalent. Get on a training program that emphasizes both strength and endurance, particularly in your arms and hands. The hands are often neglected in regular workouts, but you'll need all the strength your fingers can muster when you're using them, and sometimes not much else, to hold on to the rock wall or face.

Buying equipment is not necessary for beginners, since everything you will need is supplied. Later on, when you're getting the hang of it, a pair of rock climbing shoes will be a good purchase, since that is the piece of equipment that is most customized and fitted to its user. Don't worry about all the interesting looking equipment like carabiners and cams quite yet, but ropes and harnesses are always available for modest fees.

The reasonable price of learning to climb is one of the nicest things about it. A month-long pass to the Phoenix Rock Gym is only $40, and even a year's membership is fairly reasonable at $350. You can add family members to your pass for an additional $150 a year. This will get you and your family a whole year's worth of climbing practice, which is more than enough time to go from a flat-footed observer to a somewhat seasoned climber. But don't worry; climbing is fun on the first try and the 101st. You don't need to know much about it to enjoy yourself, and a whole weekend of climbing and related fun may be just the thing to hook you for life.

The gym is filled with 30-foot high walls with "trails" clearly marked on them. These routes are meant to simulate the various situations you might find yourself faced with on an actual rock face. The trails range in difficulty from very easy to top-notch

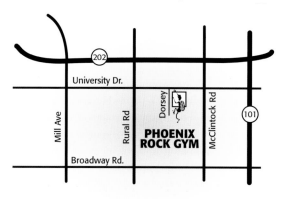

Photograph by Forest Brown

"this is impossible," depending on the number and size of holds available. A beginner's route is fairly easy to navigate as the holds are placed a reasonable distance apart, and they provide enough space to put at least a half a foot on. On the other hand, for everyone but the best climbers, a difficult route looks as though someone screwed plastic pebbles into the wall at ten-foot intervals.

During the duration of your climb, you are attached to ropes and never hanging free. Because of this fact, climbing can be a very safe activity and good for the whole family. Just keep in mind that safety is a direct product of taking care and following the directions of the more advanced climbers assisting you. Do not lose sight of the fact that you are still, after all, hanging dozens or (on the real rocks) even hundreds of feet off the ground. Make sure that you only climb with experienced, safety-conscious people—especially when learning.

The next step is, of course, to find some of these experienced people to climb with outside of the gym. Again, rock climbing isn't the kind of sport, especially at the beginner's stage, in which you just throw the gear in the back of the truck and head to the nearest cliff face. You need to do it with other people who already know what they're doing, such as guides or more experienced climbers.

There are a several ways to meet up with experienced climbers. One way is to hire them; Arizona is filled with adventure travel outfitters perfectly willing to take you climbing for a modest fee. With most companies, you'll enjoy a safe, informative, and satisfying experience. Another idea is to check the calendar of the Arizona Mountaineering Club (AMC), a Phoenix-based recreational organization that has been a presence in climbing for over thirty years. It's made up of people who love to climb just about anything that can be climbed, and their organization is an active and welcoming one. Joining the AMC only costs $25 a person, or $30 for the whole family, and it gives you access to both the Club's monthly meetings (a great time to get acquainted with climbers and learn about climbing) and their frequent

Photograph by Forest Brown

outings, which happen all over the state. The biggest benefit is that you'll be hard-pressed not to find a climbing buddy.

Events are another great way to get involved with rock climbing. The Phoenix Bouldering Competition (PBC), held for the eighteenth time in April 2001, is a competitive affair in which amazing athletes pit themselves against the kind of routes, called "problems," that punish even experts. This event is unofficially the largest of its kind and attracts some of the world's best climbers such as local three-time winner Greg Varela. The PBC is a three-day affair that brings together competition and the sheer love of the sport. Every year, the well-organized event features equipment vendors, live music, great climbing, and a ton of people interested in bouldering. Even for beginners, it's a good time and well worth checking out.

Obviously, the goal of involving yourself in rock climbing is to get on the rocks. With a proper intro-duction given at a place like the Phoenix Rock Gym, and an outing planned with a good guide service or the aficionados in the Arizona Mountaineering Club, you just might find yourself an avid member of the climbing community. Most people who climb regularly attest to the sport's addictive qualities: the physical benefits, the development of concentration and skill, and the sheer feeling of accomplishment that comes from looking down the face of a stone cliff that you just finished conquering. More so than many of the other activities described in these pages, climbing can become so addictive that it's hard to do it just once.

Directions

The Phoenix Rock Gym (PRG) is located in Tempe, AZ. From the intersection at Rural Road, go east on University Drive. PRG is located in Aztec Court on the southeast corner of University and Dorsey (halfway between Rural & McClintock). It is in the large build-ing behind the MicroTel Inn and Sunny's Pizza.

Photograph by Joel Klandrud

Outfitters

Arizona Climbing & Adventure School (see coupon pg 213), Carefree, AZ
480/363-2390, www.climbingschool.com

Arizona White-Knuckle Adventures (see coupon pg 213), Scottsdale, AZ
866/342-9669, www.arizona-adventures.com

Ascend Adventures, 800/227-2363, www.ascendadventures.com

Phoenix Rock Gym, 1353 E. University, Tempe, AZ, 480/921-8322
www.phoenixrockgym.com

For More Information

Arizona Mountaineering Club, Membership Info, P.O. Box 1695
Phoenix, AZ 85001-1695, 602/878-2485, www.azmountaineeringclub.org

Phoenix Bouldering Contest, www.phoenixboulderingcontest.org

Recommended Reading

Green, Stewart M. *Rock Climbing Arizona.* Helena, MT: Falcon Publishing, 1999.

Horst, Eric J. *Flash Training (How to Rock Climb Series).*
Helena, MT: Chockstone Press/Falcon Publishing, 1997.

Opland, Greg. *Phoenix Rock II: Rock Climbing Guide to Central Arizona Granite.*
Helena, MT: Chockstone Press/Falcon Publishing, 1998.

Photograph by Ray Bangs

146

39 Hiking Paria Canyon

282 River Crossings and Counting

Difficult
$0-$250

Imagine hiking through a canyon 2,000-feet deep and over 38 miles long. Arizona is certainly full of big canyons, but few are as narrow as Paria Canyon, starting in southern Utah and following the Paria River until it empties into the Colorado River at Lees Ferry in Arizona. Through-hiking Paria Canyon is a wild and scenic multi-day adventure for experienced hikers only. The towering canyon walls, characteristically splashed with desert varnish, feature immense red rock amphitheaters, sandstone arches, and narrow passageways, all revealing 200 million years of history. Recently, the Arizona Wilderness Act in 1984 designated Paria Canyon as a protected area, which proves that the scenery is worth the trip to this remote stretch of the Colorado Plateau.

Before starting on your 38-mile hike through this relatively tame canyon, take precautions and familiarize yourself with the possible hazards. Outdoor recreation can be dangerous and even deadly, especially when inexperienced people venture into the great wild yonder with no knowledge or preparation. In this particular area, you should be aware that there are multiple dangers to watch out for, specifically getting stuck in quicksand, being caught off-guard by a flash flood, or experiencing hypothermia or heat stroke. Combine any of these with a broken leg or ankle, and you'll be facing a life-threatening situation. Accidents can and do happen, so take your preparations seriously, and think about the consequences of stupid actions. By taking basic measures to protect yourself, risks can be minimized for a safe adventure.

The first safety precaution you can take is to hike Paria Canyon in the right season. The best times are from March to June, and again in late September to November. In order to gain a permit, you should contact the Bureau of Land Management (BLM). The cost is only $5 per day per person; only 20 hikers can start the trail each day, though, so obtaining permits is competitive. You can apply for these permits up to seven months in advance, which will help to ensure that your preferred dates are open. Dogs also require a permit and are subject to special regulations. Be aware that permits may be easier to come by in the late summer months, but you'd be crazy to hike this canyon during the rainy monsoon season. Water levels in the Narrows can jump from a trickle to over 20 feet almost instantly after a downpour. Bring hiking poles or a walking stick to check your footing, especially when you get close to the river after it has rained.

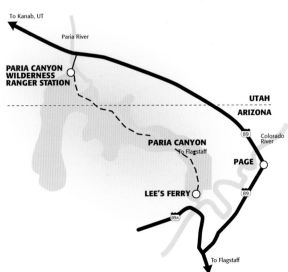

With the frequent river crossings, you are definitely going to get wet, and although hiking is available year round, the risks increase substantially during the colder months. You should always

Photograph by Ray Bangs

pack warm, dry clothes and tennis shoes or light boots with good drainage and traction. Everything in your pack should be waterproofed in plastic bags. Many backpack manufacturers sell a rain fly for your particular pack, but it's the water crossings, not the rain, that will soak your gear. Additionally, a high-quality filtration system is necessary to draw good drinking water from the springs along the way, unless you want to carry at least three gallons per person. Paria means "muddy water" in Pauite, and besides the mud, the water is likely to be contaminated with pesticides and fertilizers from upstream farms and ranches. The river is a recommended drinking source only in an emergency.

The trickiest part of planning your Paria Canyon trip is the vehicle shuttle. We highly recommend using a shuttle services to tote you and your gear to the trailhead. The average cost is approximately $100, but keep in mind that the drive one way is 75 miles. If you and a friend were going to run your own shuttle, this would mean an additional 300 vehicle miles, plus the inconvenience (and additional mileage) of driving two cars from home.

Once you have a permit, the necessary gear, and your shuttle transportation, you can sit back and enjoy this relatively easy introduction to canyoneering. Explorers have been trekking through canyons since the beginning of exploration, but only in the past few years has the sport taken off as a distinctly different aspect of hiking. Basically, like mountaineering, canyoneering is more extreme hiking, where instead of taking a leisurely stroll on a marked trail in the desert, you will be traveling through a rocky canyon. Frequently, the paths are rugged, undeveloped, and reserved for experienced hikers only. Basic climbing or rappelling gear is sometimes required. And despite the many hazards presented by canyoneering, the thrill of the backcountry experience will be rewarding.

While Paria Canyon can be an exciting destination, the hike is better known for its spectacular scenery. The route itself is only moderately challenging for most people, although the 38-mile distance can be intimidating. While 38 miles certainly doesn't sound like a weekend escape, experienced hikers have traversed the route in two long days. Three is much more manageable, while four or more allows an almost leisurely pace.

From the trailhead, it's four miles to the Narrows, which are potentially the most life-threatening section. There is no escape from a flash flood, so a good rule of thumb is to camp as high up as possible! No campfires are permitted in Paria Canyon, and the policy is to pack out what you bring in, including used toilet paper. There is no trail except the river itself, so if you follow it, you'll eventually end up at your destination. You can count the number of river crossings along the way if you like, but you might need a clicker-counter, as there are hundreds of crossings in addition to the long stretches of walking right through the river.

At 6.5 miles, Slide Rock Arch is a great photo stop. Shortly afterwards, you'll see the confluence of Buckskin Gulch. If you have time, Buckskin Gulch is a great side trip for the more advanced adventurer; the narrow slot canyon is only four feet wide in places!

Some of the other interesting spots you'll come across include Judd Hollow, The Hole, and Wrather Arch. The more time you have to spend in Paria Canyon, the more time you have to explore. Finally, the hike ends after 38 miles at Lonely Dell Ranch at Lee's Ferry.

Through-hiking Paria Canyon shouldn't be missed. Check with the rangers for weather updates and be sure to pick up a copy of the BLM guide to hiking Paria Canyon. This guide includes the basic history of the area, as well as valuable information about the location of water sources and side canyons. With good preparation, Paria Canyon is always a unique and rewarding Arizona backcountry adventure.

Directions
From Page, AZ drive northwest on US 89 towards Kanab, UT. The BLM Paria Canyon Ranger Station is located between mile markers 20 and 21. Turn left and follow the dirt road and the signs to the White House Ruins trailhead two miles south.

Shuttle Providers
Betty Price, 928/355-2252
Catalina Martinez, 928/355-2295

Outfitters
Backcountry Adventures (see coupon pg 213), 928/608-0860, www.hikinguide.com
Wild Horizons Expeditions (see coupon pg 213), 888/734-4453
   www.wildhorizonsexpd.com

For More Information
Bureau of Land Management, Arizona Strip Field Office, 345 East Riverside Drive
   St. George, UT 84790, 435/688-3230, http://paria.az.blm.gov

Recommended Reading
Kelsey, Michael. *Hiking and Exploring the Paria River.*
   Provo, UT: Kelsey Publishing, 1998.

Winter

40 Kartchner Caverns

Exploring Xanadu

Easy
$0-$250

In November 1974, two part-time cavers, Randy Tufts and Gary Tenen, discovered a narrow crack at the bottom of a sinkhole, leading deep inside the base of the Whetstone Mountains. Over the next four years, the two men explored the main cave and surrounding passages, amazed by the fragile and unique formations they saw. Having seen many vandalized, garbage-littered caves in their spelunking lives, they code-named their find Xanadu and kept it a secret as they explored.

They decided to tell James and Lois Kartchner, the property owners, about their find in 1978. The Kartchner family, after seeing the caves for themselves, agreed with Tufts and Tenen that they should be kept a secret. But as secrets often go, they knew that if word got out about the caverns or if others found them, vandalism or destruction would most likely be the outcome. They all decided that the best way to preserve the caverns would be to turn them into an official park, so negotiations with the Nature Conservancy and the Arizona State Parks Board ensued. The Kartchners then sold the area to Arizona for designation as a State Park with a guarantee that precautions would be taken to preserve its beauty. Finally, in 1988, the state legislature officially named and recognized Kartchner Caverns State Park.

After five years of intense research and survey, park development started. In 1999, twenty-five years after Tufts and Tenen's discovery, the park opened to the public. Besides the caves, the State Park offers five miles of hiking trails, including a handicapped accessible trail; a picnic area and facilities; easy trailhead access to other National Forest trails; 63 spaces in the campground with water and electric hook-up; on-site interpretive programs, and educational exhibits at the Discovery Center. The State Park entrance fee and cave tour prices are both nominal for this breathtaking below-the-ground experience. Camping is available on a first-come, first-served basis, and since the popularity of visiting the caverns keeps growing, getting there early helps ensure a site.

The cavern tour will take you through the maze of limestone caves, including the Throne and Rotunda rooms. Both rooms are nearly the size of a football field and are well worth seeing. The complete tour is 1/3-mile in length and lasts about an hour, 45 minutes of which are in the cave.

Utilizing the most advanced techniques, over a decade was spent carefully

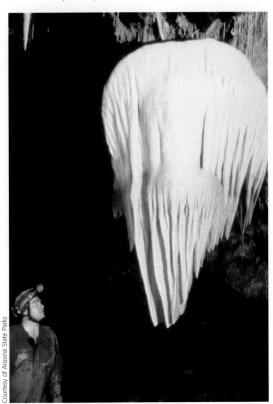

Courtesy of Arizona State Parks

Courtesy of Arizona State Parks

preparing the caves and effort was taken to minimize the detrimental effects of development. The dry, desert air is kept out by a double-door air-lock so the temperature inside the caves is held at a constant 68 degrees with 99% humidity. Walkways are dimly lit only when in use and other lights are used only intermittently to prevent overexposure or light pollution. Photography, even without a flash, is not allowed. Your guide will often remind you not to touch the cave walls, as touching or breaking the formations is punishable by law.

Tourists are not the only ones drawn to Kartchner Caverns. Every summer from April to early September, thousands of Myotis velifer bats (mostly female) return to the caverns to roost and give birth. Interestingly, this is how many caves are discovered— by the strong smell of bat guano. The guano provides essential nutrients to the cave's extremely fragile ecosystem, which includes fungi, bacteria, and insects. The bat activity is carefully monitored to limit human intrusion and ensure that roosting behavior is not severely altered.

Another unique feature about the caverns is that they are "living," because dripping water continues to deposit minerals into colorful calcified formations. One of the longest soda straw stalactites in the world is found here, measuring over 21 feet long and only a fraction of an inch in diameter. A soda straw stalactite is hollow and is still dripping water, which means it will continue growing. In startling contrast, the center of the Throne Room features a massive, towering column named "Kubla Khan." Other highlights include the world's most extensive formation of brushite moonmilk and the remains of an 80,000-year old ground sloth. The kaleidoscope of colors, dazzling formations, and such incredible variety spark the imagination and reward all visitors who tour Arizona's underground State Park.

With the popularity of the Kartchner Caverns tours, securing reservations can be difficult. Call at least a few months in advance to make sure you can get in. Reservations

are taken over the phone with a MasterCard or Visa. You can then pick up your tickets at the Park booth, but be sure to arrive at least 30 to 60 minutes before your scheduled tour. Your reservation may be cancelled 15 minutes prior to the tour time if you do not show up. If your visit to Kartchner Caverns is a last minute adventure, there's a slim chance you can slide into one of the cancelled spots, but don't count on it.

Another option is to take advantage of a pre-arranged tour conducted by Chandelle Adventure Tours. They offer tours every Thursday through the summer and every Wednesday, Thursday, and Friday from November to April. With pick up locations in Scottsdale, Phoenix, and Tucson, a Chandelle cavern tour makes for a long day, but it is an easy way to guarantee a spot on a tour. You'll be chauffeured in an air-conditioned, deluxe motorcoach, with the first segment past Tucson leading through the rolling grassland of the Empire-Cienega Conservation area. The area is strikingly beautiful and is being considered for National Monument status. Soon afterwards, you will be thankful you are not driving because the first stop may leave you a little tipsy. The visit to Elgin Winery is an opportunity to taste eight local wines and enjoy an excellent lunch. The tour continues on to Kartchner Caverns and then returns home later in the evening.

Although many environmentalists are adamantly opposed to the commercialization of Kartchner Caverns, it's hard to condemn the development with all the precautions that have been taken. Luckily, State Park designation was underway before any damage or vandalism occurred. Although it would have been incredible to experience Kartchner Caverns as Tufts and Tenen did, seeing it for the first time, it is much safer and still very interesting to take the guided tour today. It just goes to show that most secrets cannot be kept, and Xanadu is now out of the bag.

Directions

Kartchner Caverns State Park is approximately 45 minutes outside of Tucson. Take I-10 East (from Tucson) 40 miles, then exit south at exit 302 onto Hwy 90. The Park is 9 miles away on your right side.

Outfitters

Chandelle Adventure Tours (see coupon pg 213), 800/242-6335, www.azcaverntours.com

For More Information

Kartchner Caverns State Park, Benson, AZ, 520/586-2283, www.pr.state.az.us

Recommended Reading

Laine, Don & Laine, Barbara. *New Mexico & Arizona State Parks.*
     Seattle, WA: Mountaineers Books, 1998.
McClurg, David. *Adventure Of Caving.* Leavenworth, KS: D&J Press, 1996.

41 Bondurant Super-Kart School

Put the Pedal to the Metal

Easy
$100–$500+

Another droplet of sweat falls from your forehead onto your nose. The muted roar around you is hypnotic. You flex and straighten your fingers around the steering wheel, trying to relax and slow your breathing. Stay calm. You want the right timing. You rev the engine to feel its power waiting to be released, letting it out little by little. You accelerate perfectly and that puts you out in front by a nose. Suddenly you can feel that perfect harmony of mind, body, and machine putting you and keeping you in the lead until you push past the checkered flag and finally, into the victory lane. Minutes later, still reeling from the win, you walk away from your asphalt rocket and take off your helmet. One of the other drivers starts to walk over to offer his hand in congratulations. In awe, he flips up his helmet visor and respectfully says, "Nice driving, Mom!"

Go-karts are supposedly for kids, but Bob Bondurant knew when starting his Super-Kart School that there were a lot of kids out there—they just happened to be a few years older. Bondurant's adrenaline-packed super-kart programs feature the top-of-the-line KGB Spy Shifter Super-Karts with Kawasaki 125cc motors. They provide superior handling and high-speed performance guaranteed to leave your body imprint in the seat. Even

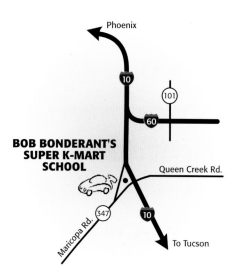

with only 32 horsepower, they corner at 2.5 Gs and reach a top speed of 120 mph. These are not your typical run-of-the-mill go-karts!

Bondurant only has a few requirements for his students. First, every student (and all the fans you bring to watch you) will be required to sign waivers and releases. Minors must also have a parental waiver. Secondly, as with all active travel and recreation, you should be in good physical condition. Racing with a weak heart would definitely not be a good idea—it needs to keep pace with all the action!

Once you have filled out the appropriate paperwork, Bondurant will outfit you with a helmet, karting suit, rib protector, gloves, and neck collar. Now you're ready to learn the fundamentals, including correct seat and body positioning, accelerating, shifting, steering, and proper braking techniques. If you start with the basic two-hour course, you'll gradually build up your skills until you are ready to take off on your own.

The better option is to go for the longer, half-day course where you'll learn the fundamental skills mentioned above plus cornering techniques and beginning race theory. Taking a longer course means more training and, of course, more time in the kart. The full-day program dives even deeper into advanced line technique and race theory to improve your smoothness, consistency, and overall control. The instructors emphasize picking your line on the track and then executing it. Soon this becomes automatic. Super-Kart School actually makes you a better driver both on the racetrack and in city traffic; road hazards can be avoided easier as your reactions become quicker and more

Photograph by Rick Scuteri

instinctive. That's all good and true when you are signing up, but really, who cares about the road; here, out on the track, you'll become a monster!

If you really want to go crazy (i.e., thinking about trading in your car for a super-kart), the advanced courses feature one-on-one instruction with professional super-kart racing champions. Super-karting is serious business at Bonderant's. You can even enroll in a two-day advanced course for double the track time to hone your skills. By then you'll be unstoppable and likely to quit your day job.

If you're not convinced that a little shifter kart will give you enough spunk, you can try out one of the bigger tracksters in the Bondurant stable. Bob Bondurant's School of High Performance Driving, which came into existence long before the super-karts, is highly respected and keeps growing in popularity every year. If car movies and chase scenes instill a burning desire to strap in behind the wheel of a screaming road machine, here's your opportunity to go as fast as you'll ever want to go. Paul Newman, Clint Eastwood, David Hasselhoff, and Tom Cruise are just a handful of the celebrities who have graduated from the School. Bondurant's is considered the best and with the growing popularity of Arizona as a location for blockbuster movies, there's a chance you might be driving head-to-head with your favorite Hollywood action hero.

As your interest grows, you can try out other vehicles from Bondurant's fleet of full-sized speed machines. His stable of cars is very impressive with over 150 customized Ford vehicles, assuring that every student has their own set of wheels. All the Bondurant racecar programs are designed for maximum minutes on the track, so you'll be getting what is known in the racing world as more seat-time. So if you have the means and desire to drive a racecar, sign right up. You won't be disappointed. Driving courses are offered year round, seven days a week. You can choose from two, three, or four-day courses, which begin every Monday and Thursday. If you just want to put the pedal to the metal once, with minimal instruction, or are looking for a basic introduction to see how you like it, short courses are offered at limited times throughout the year.

While the big cars are exciting, driving racecars is not a cheap hobby nor is the Bondurant racing experience. The High-Performance driving two-day course runs just under $2,000, and $3,000 for the three-day course, making for one of the most expensive weekends. First-timers can spend almost $4,000 for the four-day Grand Prix Road Racing program. This does not even include racecar insurance, hotel, meals, or transportation to the track. Like we said before, going to a Bondurant School is serious business and serious fun. If that is way out of your price range, the super-karts are a much more reasonable option for a splash-and-go shot of speed. The two-hour super-kart course is only $150 while half-day programs start at $275. Even the most advanced two-day program is just over $1,600. Although a less expensive alternative, the go-karts are by no means a cheaper experience than the big brother versions. The two-hour shifter cart course is offered on Tuesday, Wednesday, and Thursday of each week. The half-day and full-day courses are offered on Friday, Saturday, and Sunday. Call to check for course availability.

If all this hype hasn't swayed your interests enough, imagine this scenario… You're out for a couple beers with some friends, when one starts bragging about his screaming-fast summit of Humphreys Peak. Another chimes in about how she recently completed her freefall skydiving course. Everyone takes turns until it comes around to you. To keep up and maintain your cool, you simply say, "Well, I've climbed Humphreys pretty fast, I've jumped out of planes a couple times, and I've even gone kayaking, but the best was going from 0 to 100 in about six seconds." You take a casual sip of your drink for dramatic effect and then add, "in a go-kart."

Directions

Bondurant's Super-Kart School is located south of Phoenix at the Firebird International Raceway. From Phoenix follow I-10 south towards Tucson. Exit on Hwy 347 west (Maricopa Rd). The School will be on the right.

For More Information

Bondurant's Super-Kart School, 20000 S. Maricopa Road, Gate 3, Chandler, AZ
    800/842-7223, www.bondurant.com

Recommended Reading

Assael, Shaun. *Wide Open.* New York, NY: Ballantine Books, 1999.
McCullough, Bob. *My Greatest Day in Nascar: The Legends of Auto Racing Recount Their Greatest Moments.* New York, NY: Griffin Trade Paperback, 2001.

Wings Over Willcox
The Flight of the Cranes

Easy
$0–$250

As you crouch in the grass, ready to fire, you're momentarily stunned by the beauty of the birds—their wide wings spread out against each other, their necks extended before them slanting up into the sky. It's almost enough to make you forget the task at hand. Almost.

You pull your head together just in time to focus in on two of them, layered over one another in the air, flying through your sight. You suck in a breath, steady your hands, and…Click. Got 'em. That's a keeper, you think as you wind to the next frame and prepare for the follow-up journal duty. As a birder, you know to record the date, time, species and location in your log, so you won't ever forget the first time you saw a sandhill crane.

Arizona is home to thousands of species of birds, from tiny buzzing hummingbirds to majestic falcons and harriers. The state's rich diversity of climates allows for a huge variety of animal life, and the bird population is proof of it. You can find interesting species in your backyard on a good day, or travel up and down the state taking in the incredible array of avian life one region at a time. Birding is a big deal in Arizona, simply because you can do it so close to home and still experience different populations each time you go out.

Birdwatchers, contrary to popular conception, do not just sit in the bushes and wait to see what flies by. They seek the birds the way a hunter seeks the prey, but their method of "attack" is somewhat different. When a new, feathered friend is spotted, the trusty old notebook is opened up and the sighting is recorded. Birdwatchers even keep score and rate themselves against each other. In order to add more rare birds to one's notebook, it is necessary to beat the bush a little, to journey into the wilderness, and to seek out some of the more shy species, rather than just sitting on a rock by a lake, reading *Walden*, and waiting for them to fly by.

There are many birding events in Arizona, and even if you're new to the whole thing, you shouldn't be afraid to attend any one of them. After all, every experienced birder has been right where you are—holding a blank book, waiting to fill it up. Just go out and have fun. Bring a pair of binoculars for spotting, and don't forget your camera. You want your non-birding friends to be able to see a photo of what you're talking about when you babble excitedly about the elegant trogon you saw over the weekend.

For your first birding event, you might want to try Wings Over Willcox (WOW), a festival going into its ninth year in 2002. Willcox is located in Cochise County, a region that is home to more than 500 avian species. The area is also known for its rich history; Cochise, the Apache chief who successfully drove the U.S. Army out of Arizona in 1861,

made his base in the Dragoon Mountains southwest of present-day Willcox. Fort Bowie, a center of military operations in the late 1800s, is also close by.

But the birds command the stage during the Wings weekend. The festival takes place in the middle of January, when thousands of sandhill cranes leave their summer grounds in Alaska and Siberia and set up winter roost in the

Photograph by Paul & Joyce Berquist

Sulphur Springs Valley. Seeing the cranes return from their morning feeding is a highlight of the three-day festival; for birders just getting started, this is a great chance to see a phenomenon straight out of "Wild Kingdom." Thousands of cranes flock to the spot, one of the biggest crane roosts in the state, and reward diligent spectators with their presence.

Crane watching is not the only point of the weekend, though. Throughout the course of the event, there are hawk stalks, sparrow seeks, owl prowls, and various other cleverly named birding jaunts going on, as well as informative lectures, slide shows, and dinner talks about birds and birding. You can also indulge your interest in geology, natural science, or photography, as there are educational seminars in these areas as well. In all, it is an informative three days, and a good chance to get connected with the Arizona birding community.

There are a few facts to keep in mind if you're planning on coming out for the Willcox festival, most notably in regard to the weather. Willcox is located in the mountains, and as such, unlike Phoenix and other desert spots, January can be quite chilly.

The temperatures during your morning expeditions will probably dip to around twenty degrees, so bring appropriate clothing or else you might find yourself shaking too hard to hold your binoculars steady.

If you enjoy Wings over Willcox, or you wanted to make it out and simply could not for one reason or another, there are plenty of other birding opportunities to take advantage of. Your best connection to these other events is through the Southeastern Arizona Bird Observatory (SABO), a non-profit organization dedicated to conserving the birds and habitats of the southeastern region of Arizona surrounding Willcox. They sponsor seminars and expeditions year-round, and though they have only been around since 1996, they sponsor quite a few larger activities every year.

If you are visiting from out of state, get in touch with them and see what's going on during the time of your stay. If you are a native Arizonan, stay informed and support their efforts through participation. Anyone is welcome to join, and if the condition of the state's bird population is important to you, it is a good cause. Members are also entitled to discounts on the various events SABO sponsors, as well as an informative quarterly newsletter.

Birding combines numerous outdoor activities and skills—hiking, photography, and nature identification. And since there's always some new specimen needing to be looked up in your trusty Audubon Guide, it is a great way to experience nature. It is the perfect wilderness experience for detectives, for observers, and for those who want something more to do during the hike from point A to point B.

Directions

To get to Willcox from Tucson take I-10 East to exit 336, the I-10 business route. This road becomes I-10/AZ 186. Stewart Street will be on your left. The Willcox Community Center, where the registration for WOW is held, is located on this road. The folks there can tell you where to go for other birding events.

For More Information

Southeastern Arizona Bird Observatory, Bisbee, AZ, 520/432-1388
    www.sabo.org
Willcox Chamber of Commerce and Agriculture, Willcox, AZ, 800/200-2272
    www.willcoxchamber.com

Recommended Reading

Gray, Mary Taylor. *Watchable Birds of the Southwest.*
    Missoula, MT: Mountain Press Publishing Company, 1995.
Kaufman, Lynn Hassler. *Birds of the American Southwest.*
    Tucson, AZ: Rio Nuevo Publishers, 2000.
Rappole, John H. *Birds of the Southwest: Arizona, New Mexico, Southern California
    & Southern Nevada.* College Station, TX: Texas A&M University Press, 2001.

RVs and Roadtrips

Your Tent on Wheels

Easy
$250-$500+

From the World's Largest Kokopelli to elaborate shrines to trading posts, roadside attractions are a fundamental part of America's highway history. As soon as people started driving long distances, enterprising, slightly bent people started trying to figure out ways to make them pull over and pay a modest fee to see something outrageous or just plain weird. There are numerous stops all along our Arizona highways and backroads, and the list grows the more miles you cover. On this kind of adventure there is just one rule—pull over when the signs tell you to.

The best way to take this kind of weekend road trip is from the captain's chair of your very own rented RV. Don't worry, this is not as hard as it might sound; renting an RV is a fairly easy proposition, as dealers are located across the state. When you set out to rent, keep in mind that for a short weekend trip, a small, class C RV (one with a "cab-over" bed) is perfectly suitable. It's also a bit cheaper, on average, than the larger class A RV

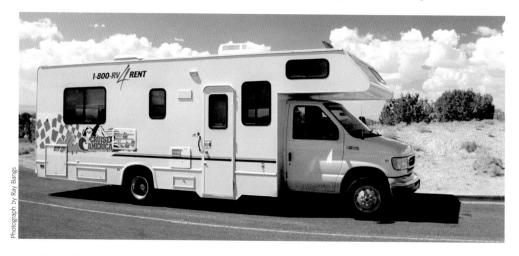

Photograph by Ray Bangs

(one that resembles a bus), since the A is generally bigger and consumes more gas. But if you've got the kids in tow, it is worth the few extra bucks to give everyone more room to move and to get away from your potentially noisy passengers.

Since RVs are big, expensive pieces of equipment, plan to leave a pretty hefty deposit. And though we shouldn't need to say it, don't vandalize the vehicle. Not only does it hurt the dealer's chances of ever selling the thing (or even renting it again), it'll cost you. Remember, they've got around five hundred of your bucks and a credit card number. If you're not foolish, you'll get your whole deposit back, so be sure to check the rental policies thoroughly. Three-night rentals start around $400, but go up in price based on the size of the RV and the time of year. There are often hidden charges, so be sure to ask about the different costs and get it all in writing. The adventure might seem expensive, but if you add up what three nights at a hotel would cost, the sticker shock drops considerably.

Once you're in your new weekend home, just pick up a map and start driving. It should not take you long before you come across attractions that can be labeled "unusual and bizarre." Route 66 is particularly famous for this sort of thing; even today, a tour of

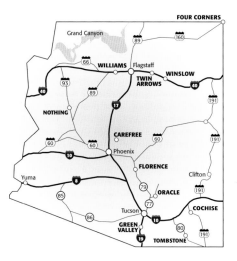

"the Mother Road" will put you in contact with some certifiably strange sights, as well as a surprising number of great restaurants and diners. You'll hit everything from the Museum Club (a.k.a. The Zoo), one of Arizona's best-known bars, to the elegant La Posada Hotel in Winslow, a National Historic Landmark. Built between 1928 and 1930, La Posada became the Santa Fe Railway's base lodging and the finest little hotel in the state. The hotel is still open to guests, and the prices are more than reasonable given the lavish accommodations.

But let's not get too cultured. Make sure your home-on-wheels finds its way off the beaten track and onto some of the state's lesser-known backroads. Once you're off the main roads, you'll find attractions like Biosphere 2 in Oracle, where science tried and failed to create a self-sustaining environment, a possible forerunner of independent space colonies. Or you can see "The Thing" in Cochise, the what-in-the-world-is-this central exhibit in a tin-shack museum that also boasts a car Hitler may have ridden in. "The Thing" was reportedly found in a nearby cave, mummified—and very spooky.

Arizona is filled with roadside attractions. Obviously, the more mysterious these sites are, the more interesting, so here's a list to write down and check off during your statewide RV run. We'll leave it to you to find them, see them, and take the pictures you'll show (or won't show) to your friends and relatives. You may not hit them all in one weekend, but it is possible.

1. Drive into Twin Arrows.
2. Visit the world's largest Kachina doll in Carefree.
3. Play the childhood ball game foursquare at the Four Corners, where Arizona, New Mexico, Colorado, and Utah meet at a single point.
4. Stop at the Tom Mix Death Site Marker, seventeen miles south of Florence, where the famous silent-film cowboy met his end when a suitcase struck him in the head after he drove into a gully.
5. Tour the Titan II Missile Museum in Green Valley, which is a decommissioned Cold War missile silo that provides tours and insights courtesy of retired missile personnel.
6. Visit the town of Nothing—Population: about 4 (including dogs).
7. Visit the Merman at the Birdcage Theater or the World's Biggest Rosebush, all while you're in Tombstone reliving the glory of the Old West.
8. Experience life with the Flintstones in a reproduction Bedrock in Valle, near Williams.
9. Communicate with the Lord, who frequents a pint-sized church near Yuma.
10. See the multitude of sights on Route 66.

If you exhaust this list, contact www.roadsideamerica.com to get more roadside sightseeing information. You will be amazed at what is out there.

Do it right, and your RV journey into the heart of Arizona's strangeness will end up being one of the most memorable trips you will ever take. Just remember to keep an open mind and stop whenever the urge strikes you. Don't set a time schedule or plan on

being anywhere at a certain time; just let the road take you, let the sights guide you, and they will. It'll be the first stress-free vacation you've ever taken, the only one for which no itinerary is the best itinerary. All you have to do is drive between the dots of interest, and gawk at what you find there.

Directions

There are RV dealers located throughout the state. Call the one closest to you for directions. Once you're on the road, any road atlas, combined with a rough knowledge of where the points of attraction are, will serve you just fine.

Outfitters

Cruise America (see coupon pg 213), 11 West Hampton Ave., Mesa, AZ
    480/464-7300, www.cruiseamerica.com

Messner RV Rentals (see coupon pg 215), Phoenix, AZ, 800/561-9662
    www.messnerrv.im-ltd.com

For More Information

Roadside America, www.roadsideamerica.com

Roadside Peek, www.roadsidepeek.com

Recommended Reading

Cohen, Korene C. *Museums & Other Attractions of Arizona's Smaller Communities.*
    Tucson, AZ: Dancing Unicorn Press, 1992.

Kirby, Doug; Smith, Ken; & Wilkins, Mike. *The New Roadside America: The Modern*
    Traveler's Guide to the Wild and Wonderful America's Tourist Attractions.
    New York, NY: Fireside, 1992.

Neuner, John D. *Arizona Myths, Fallacies and Misconceptions.*
    New York, NY: First Leaf Publishing, 2001.

Photography Seminars
More Than Just Snapshots

What separates your snapshots from the photographic art found in *Arizona Highways* magazine? Have you ever dreamed about being hired on assignment for *National Geographic*? Professional photography is a difficult business, especially with the wealth of stock images available and the large number of professionals competing for a limited number of spots. So although you may never have your photos printed in a preeminent photography publication, there are still ways to transform your snapshots into photos with more substance.

The first, easiest, and least expensive way to start is to go to the library and check out a dozen books on how to take better pictures. You will find titles on light, film, the "rule of thirds," and equipment, as well as photography books focused on studio work, landscapes, animals, sports, adventure travel, etc. Read, read, read and soon enough, with plenty of practice, you'll start seeing the better pictures, and you'll start getting better slides and prints as a result.

The second way to become a skilled photographer is simply to take more pictures. If you are using anything other than the most economically priced film, however, your hobby can quickly become unaffordable. A good rule of thumb to follow is that you should get at least one good photo out of every roll or two. The professional photographer assigned to a feature story for *National Geographic* may shoot more than one thousand rolls of film! If you have a personal computer, though, one alternative is to use a digital camera. Film processing requires so many chemicals that a digital camera, which stores images on a floppy disk or memory card, is very eco-friendly. Digital cameras are initially pricier to purchase, but you'll never have to buy film again. Photos taken with a higher-end digital camera, combined with some masterful manipulation and retouching in Photoshop, can quickly create an online photo album to be very proud of. Digital cameras with enough resolution can also produce images that can be blown up to an impressive 8" x 10" or even larger. However, unless you are using the professional quality (and professional priced) digital gear, these photos will probably not be seen in any magazines in the near future.

The third way to turn your photos into more than just snapshots is to take classes or workshops. Although this is the most expensive of the three options, learning from professionals is the best way to go. Your first option here would be to take a photography class at a local university or community college, but most of these courses are spent inside the classroom. This won't really help you if you want to learn landscape or wildlife photography. So if you want to take portraits, go to a studio and learn to take portraits. Likewise, if you want to take pictures of outdoor landscapes, you must get out in the

Photograph by Jack McAward

field with people who specialize in outdoor landscapes.

As a non-profit branch of the magazine, the Friends of Arizona Highways conducts photography workshops throughout the year, ranging from one-day classes to weeklong backcountry adventures. Whether you are an amateur or a seasoned pro, each course provides instruction in a small group setting with an Arizona Highways photo-grapher. Photographers who have taught recent seminars include big names like Gary Ladd, Marc Muench, George Stocking, and David Elms. Learning from these well-respected pros will give your picture-taking skills a serious boost. All lodging, transportation, lunches, and entrance fees are also included, so students can concentrate on creating pictures. Some of the recent workshop topics have included the wildflowers of the Rockies and various caves in southern Arizona, Monument Valley, and Canyon de Chelly.

Even though the longer, five-day trips will give you more practice and are very reasonably priced, the two-day workshops are actually the best value. For less than $100, you will receive several hours of evening classroom instruction with a pro right at the Arizona Highways office followed by an on location photo shoot at popular sites such as Flagstaff, Jerome, the Desert Botanical Gardens, or the Phoenix Zoo. Some of the courses, including Photography for Publication, allow a behind-the-scenes look at the magazine's operation.

Women seeking to become the next Annie Leibovitz of Southwest scenery should check out the Arizona Outdoors Woman (AOW) calendar. This organization, which offers a variety of activities from Tai Chi to llama trekking, provides one-day photo classes taught by experts in a friendly environment. The day-long classes range from $20-$60 dollars and all skill levels are welcome to attend.

Another Arizona company, Windwalker Expeditions, provides an opportunity to take exciting photos by combining photography with horseback riding, archaeological tours, camping trips, and jeep tours. Jack McAward and his Sonoran Desert Guides will escort you into areas of central Arizona that are full of scenic landscapes and help you visually develop a photo even before you set the camera on the tripod. By seeing a photo before you shoot it, your less-than-spectacular pictures can be taken to the next level.

Jack McAward specializes in horseback adventures that possess excellent (as he likes to say) "picture-making" potential. The half-day Desert Botanical Tour is a grand introduction to the diverse flora of the Sonoran desert. The five to six-hour Indian Ruin Tour

167

Courtesy of Arizona Outdoors Woman

promises adventure while cantering through a land full of ancient ruins. If you are looking for something a little longer, Jack offers photography camps for those seeking to really concentrate on learning the skills (and tricks) of the trade. With spacious tents and gourmet meals, a photo tour with Windwalker Expeditions is a magnificent way to spend three days and two nights exploring the Sonoran desert and sleeping under the stars.

Whether you start out by reading all the books on photography you can, taking a college class, or jumping right in on a photo tour, remember that becoming a better photographer takes time, practice, and patience. One weekend is not going to transform you into Ansel Adams, but if you turn all your weekend escapes into opportunities to make better pictures, soon enough, the roll of film you get back from the photo lab will be more than just snapshots.

Directions
Evening classes are held at the Friends of Arizona Highways office located at 2039 W. Lewis Avenue. For other outfitters, call and ask for directions to their location.

Outfitters
Arizona Outdoors Woman (see coupon pg 215), 602/375-1054
    www.azoutdoorswoman.com
Friends of Arizona Highways (see coupon pg 215), 888/790-7042
    www.friendsofazhighways.com
Windwalker Expeditions (see coupon pg 215), 888/785-3382, 480/585-3382
    www.windwalkerexpeditions.com

Recommended Reading
Arizona On My Mind. Guilford, CT: Globe Piquot Press, 1996.
Lange, Joseph. *Photographer's Guide to the Grand Canyon and Northern Arizona.*
    Mechanicsburg, PA: Stackpole Books, 2001.

45 Arizona Snowbowl
Skiing Above the Saguaros

| Medium |
| $0–$250 |

Snow in the desert? Yes, it's true. Arizona offers excellent skiing and snowboarding. Any traveler who arrives during the winter months should come prepared to hit the slopes. The Arizona Snowbowl, just 135 miles north of Phoenix, possesses the quality of runs and convenient location to make it the most popular ski destination in Arizona. The resort is located in scenic Flagstaff, which is a beautiful little college town with character to spare. Besides the abundance of great restaurants and bars, its alpine atmosphere is more reminiscent of Colorado than the desert Southwest.

Snowbowl lies at the top of the San Francisco Peaks, an isolated mountain range formed by the same volcanic forces that blew up Mount St. Helens in the early 1980s. The San Francisco Peaks are a part of the Colorado Plateau, which also contains the Grand Canyon and Canyonlands National Park. The mountains were subjected to human abuse for the first half of the twentieth century, primarily through mismanaged logging, mining, and livestock grazing. Since the 1960s, conservation efforts have largely succeeded in re-establishing the natural state of the area, and the effects of clear-cutting and overgrazing have largely disappeared. Mining has recently been stopped in the mountains as well, and a proposal is under review by the federal government to designate the area as a Traditional Cultural Property, based on the fact that at least thirteen Native American tribes see the San Francisco Peaks as a sacred place. This proposal would ban mining in the Peaks forever and preserve the area in its current, natural state.

Courtesy of Arizona Office of Tourism

After spending a lot of time in Arizona's desert, the drive into Flagstaff, among the ponderosa pines and junipers, is a refreshing change. We can tell you for sure that there is nothing quite like leaving saguaro-strewn Phoenix in the morning and seeing snow three hours later. It's more proof of the fact that Arizona offers something for every taste, literally across all four seasons.

Obviously, given Arizona's desert reputation, most out-of-state visitors forget their gear at home.

Courtesy of Arizona Office of Tourism

The rental equipment at Snowbowl is well maintained, so you can ski or snowboard without worrying about pop-out bindings, gouged skis and decks, or blister-raising boots. High-performance gear is available too, so expert skiers can rent without taking a quality reduction. Be sure to get to the mountain early in the morning if you're renting, though, since equipment goes out on a first-come, first-served basis, and you cannot call ahead to reserve gear. If you prefer to just show up at the mountain with your gear ready to go, there are a few other shops in town that rent quality equipment. Call ahead to find the best gear at the best prices.

Snowbowl's elevation is 11,500 feet at the top of Aggasiz, the highest chair lift, and even higher at the top of the foot-traffic-only Upper Bowl. There are thirty-five runs to choose from, and most of them are conveniently grouped on the mountain by skill level. If you're a beginner, for example, and take the Hart Prairie lift, you won't find yourself making a wrong turn and taking on a double black diamond instead of the quiet, gentle hill you were anticipating. The newest skiers on the mountain will have fun on the network of greens at the bottom of the hill, while intermediate skiers will find more challenging terrain on the other side of the lower mountain.

At the highest elevations, however, advanced skiers will not be disappointed. Snowbowl offers ample challenges for the expert, from sweet mogul-strewn runs like Tiger and Casino, to the Upper Bowl, a backcountry area accessible only by hiking. Once there, you'll know the trek was worth it, as the grade is steep, and the Bowl gets the best snow on the mountain.

Another note for the experts—keep your eye out for unmarked trails. There are a few running directly under the lifts that are among the best trails on the mountain for challenging terrain. Look down as you're taking Aggasiz to the top, and you'll see what we mean. There are even runs through the trees, which shortcut all the major expert trails. Just keep your eyes open.

Snowbowl caters to the snowboarder set too. North Star is the mountain's snowboard park, complete with a half-pipe and enough jumps and bumps to make any boarder happy. Every trail on the mountain is open to snowboards as well, except for Southern Belle, a skiers-only intermediate.

If your trip to Flagstaff happens to fall outside of ski season, don't fret. Snowbowl is open all year round, with hiking boots replacing skis and boards as the grass turns green. The scenic skyride is open all summer too, and riding the chair on a clear July day gives you spectacular views of the San Francisco Peaks mountain range that surrounds you, as well as incredible views of picturesque Flagstaff below. For more information on hiking the area, contact the Flagstaff Visitor's Center or the San Francisco Peaks Ranger's district office. Both organizations are well versed in hiking the area and can point you in the right direction based on your experience and skill level.

During the ski season, Snowbowl is open from 9 a.m. to 4 p.m. Get there early and enjoy the entire day on the mountain. Because it's a relatively small ski area, one seven-hour day will do just fine, but the terrain is varied enough to easily keep you interested for two or three days. Once you've taken off the boots and soaked in your hotel jacuzzi, head out into Flagstaff for the evening to enjoy a little dinner and maybe some après-ski nightlife; the town hops, especially when school is in session at Northern Arizona University. The next day, you can head home refreshed with your snow fix fully satisfied. Now you can tell everyone that Arizona isn't just for desert rats—the snow bunnies hang out there, too.

Directions

From the I-17/I-40 Junction south of Flagstaff, go north 1.8 miles on Milton Rd. (I-17 becomes Milton and Milton becomes Route 66.) Proceed under the train bridge and follow the curve towards the east. At the first stoplight, turn left onto Humphreys St. (Hwy 180). Proceed on Humphreys for .6 miles to Ft. Valley Road. Turn left on Ft. Valley Road (Hwy 180) and proceed 6.8 miles to the Arizona Snowbowl road turn off. Ski Lift Lodge is located at this intersection. Turn right onto Snowbowl Road and proceed approximately 7 miles up the mountain to reach Hart Prairie Lodge. Aggasiz Lodge is approximately .3 miles beyond Hart Prairie Lodge. Please drive carefully on Snowbowl Road as there are steep grades, winding roads, and wildlife in this area.

For More Information

Arizona Snowbowl Ski Area, Flagstaff, AZ, 928/779-1951, www.arizonasnowbowl.com
Flagstaff Visitor's Center, 800/842-7293
San Francisco Peaks Ranger's District Office, 928/526-0866

Recommended Reading

Leocha, Charles A. *Ski America and Canada: Top Winter Resorts in the U.S.A. and Canada.* Boston, MA: World Leisure, 2000.
Miller, Warren. *Ski and Snow Country: The Golden Years of Skiing in the West, 1930s-1950s.* Portland, OR: Graphic Arts Center Publishing Company, 2000.
Shelton, Peter et al. *The Unofficial Guide to Skiing in the West.* New York, NY: Hungry Minds Inc., 1999.

Verde Hot Springs

The Bottomless Tub

People once flocked to hot springs for a variety of reasons, but mostly it was to focus on the therapeutic benefits of a warm bath. At one time, doctors even prescribed a good soaking in mineral rich, heated water as a treatment for many ailments. However, since the invention of the Jacuzzi, relatively few Americans take the time to enjoy this natural, relaxing luxury. Fortunately for those of you who still savor this kind of healthy experience, Arizona is home to dozens of these natural Jacuzzis, with one of the best found in the Verde Valley.

During the early 1900s, many hot springs were developed in the eastern U.S., but with the outbreak of World War I, interest faded in this leisure activity. Finally, in the 1920s, one Arizona hot spring resort sprung up on the Verde River about 20 miles west of the town of Strawberry. Frequently used by the Tonto Apaches for medicinal purposes and known to early explorers as the "Indian Curing Waters," the Verde Hot Spring Resort quickly became surprisingly trendy. Despite the initial craze, the location was virtually impossible to reach. Luckily, however, the new Fossil Creek roadway was soon completed and business was booming as visitors from around the country flocked to the resort. Unfortunately, its success was short-lived, and by World War II, the resort was nearly abandoned. Years later, an attempt was made to restore the Verde Hot Spring Resort to its original glory, but the plans just did not work out. Finally, in 1962, the remains of the hotel burned to the ground. Today, the walkway and the foundation serve as the only reminders of the popular retreat.

Today, half the fun of the going to the Verde River Hot Spring is getting there. The

drive is one of the most scenic in Arizona—you can see a long way down! The route winds gently past the turn off to the Fossil Springs trailhead, but shortly afterward, it becomes steep and narrow. The bumpy gravel road is cut into the side of the mountain and no guardrail protects you from plummeting hundreds or even thousands of feet if you go over the edge. Low clearance vehicles including most passenger cars can manage the terrain; however, 4WD is recommended due to the few difficult sections. When you finally descend to the river elevation, you'll see a second Fossil Springs turn off and a power plant on the right, but keep going. You'll cross a bridge and on most days, several vehicles will be parked just off the road. The Fossil Creek drainage provides excellent swimming and a great way to cool off in the summer. Keep in mind that this once-secret swimming hole now gets crowded on the weekends.

Stay left where the road branches north and leads to Camp Verde. Forest Service signs point the way to Childs Power Plant and the Verde River. The road dead-ends at the camping area. After choosing a spot and setting up camp, many people like to cool off with a swim. Water sandals or old tennis shoes are a must for the hike to the spring and are recommended even for swimming. You'll see a group of waterfalls hidden in the thick

Photograph by Ray Bangs

bullrushes just upriver of the campground if you stay along the right (eastern) shore. Don't be surprised to see a fellow camper sitting in a lawn chair placed in the shallow water and reading a book. The water flowing through here from the power plant is exceptionally cool and refreshing as compared to the main section of the Verde River.

The mile walk to the springs is rather easy, but can be scorching in the summer. Bring ample drinking water, wear a hat and sunglasses, and don't forget to lather on the sunscreen. Ask another camper to show you the trail to the hot spring, as it can sometimes be difficult to find. If nobody else knows or if you are lucky enough to have the campground to yourself (not likely), walk to the northeast or top of the camping area. When you find the trail, walk across the bridge and follow the signs to the old dirt road, which soon descends to the river. Cross the river towards the foundation and ruins of the burned-down resort, and you'll see the walkway leading directly to the spring.

If you are feeling more daring, you can just walk upriver from the campground. This is a significantly shorter route, but it can be tricky in places. Keep a close watch on rapids or deep water holes, and when on shore, avoid the thorn-covered blackbrush and bothersome prickly plants. When you reach the hot springs, you'll have to scramble up the cliff to the walkway. The climbing is not technical or incredibly challenging, but it is a lot more difficult than following the paved path of the first route.

The water at the source of the hot spring is about 104° F, but cools to 96° F in the outer pool during winter. You definitely feel better after a good soak during any season. The early resort owners even claimed that drinking the hot spring's high mineral content water was especially good for stomachaches, indigestion, and kidney problems. For a short stretch of time, water from the Verde River Hot Spring was bottled and sold in pharmacies. The tingling effervescence of a soak is usually enough healing for most people, however, some bring a portable water filter and fill an empty jug or two. Although no problems arising from drinking the water have been reported, a daily multivitamin is probably a better idea!

The main pool is big enough for several people and offers stunning views of the river and mountains. Your feet rest on the walls tapering in so you will be not standing on the bottom. A second pool is enclosed by stone walls and a tarped roof. Off-color cartoons, interesting quotes, and modern-day petroglyphs cover the inside of the walls, so soaking in this tub means at least a few laughs. Check out the caves cut into the side of the cliff and you will find more pools enveloped in darkness. Although offering privacy, the caves are somewhat difficult to maneuver in and their pools are not the best for soaking. While the main pool is the most natural, the most comfortable, and the most scenic, the sun can make soaking in this hot tub a very toasty experience. If you get too warm or uncomfortable, take a dip and cool off in the Verde River.

Although a sign seen on the drive in prohibits nudity, the Verde River Hot Spring is popular with naturalists. Since the springs are remotely located, many choose to soak and sunbathe nude, but bring a swimsuit just in case others object. Likewise, if you're the swimsuit-wearing type, don't be surprised by some visitors' clothing optional policy. Whether you go naked or not, be sure to pack out all your trash and any you might see. Overall, spending a weekend by the beautiful Verde River is a wonderful, healthy, and refreshing experience.

Directions

From Strawberry (near Payson) on AZ Hwy 87, turn west on Fossil Creek Road. The campground is approximately 18 miles. Stay left for the entire trip, watch for the signs, and drive carefully.

For More Information

Coconino National Forest, Verde Ranger District, 300 E. Hwy 260, Camp Verde, AZ 928/567-4121, www.fs.fed.us/r3/coconino

Recommended Reading

Bischoff, Matt. *Touring Arizona Hot Springs.* Helena, MT: Falcon Publishing, 1999.
Slingluff, Jim. *Verde River Recreation Guide.* Phoenix, AZ: Golden West Publishers, 1990.

Aerial Combat

I Feel the Need for Speed

Medium
$250-$500+

When the new bogey suddenly buzzed by on my left, I didn't think about him too much; I was too concerned about the one on my tail, guns blazing, aiming to shoot down my plane at any moment. So all I could do was roll to my right and hope for the best…and that's what I did, except the best didn't happen. Next thing I know, I'm hot, smoking, and the guy sitting behind me is getting roasted by an engine fire. Now the second bogey is coming around to finish me, as if the flames coming from my intakes aren't good enough for him. Not my day at all, I'd say. But I'm not on the ground yet. So I wheel it around, coming back hard left, pull this first target into my sights, take aim, and…

Fighter Combat International (FCI) is an organization that operates year-round out of Williams Gateway Airport in Mesa, east of downtown Phoenix. For the price of admission, they give civilians the chance to actually take the controls of a German-built acrobatic aircraft and perform some of the breathtaking tricks—barrel rolls, inverted spins, tumbles—that make air show audiences gasp. If you choose to, you can operate the controls for up to 75 percent of the flight, giving the stick over only when you take off and land. You'll get to be Maverick (or Iceman, if prefer) for a day, executing moves and creating a memory sure to stay with you after the rest of your mind has gone to goo.

If that isn't cool enough for you, get this—if you round up some friends to go up with you, the group of you can actually engage in air combat, using sophisticated laser weapon simulators, smoke generators, and on-board combat sound cards. Practice up beforehand on the video games and if you're lucky, you can shoot down your best friend in mid air, and then impress them all with a perfect inverted spin.

FCI has been around since 1997, and just recently moved its base of operations to Williams Gateway. Its instructors are all experienced pilots with decades of military and aerobatic flying experience, and they are dedicated to delivering the most exhilarating adventure to each and every one of their customers. This adventure does, unfortunately, have a few physical guidelines that might keep some participants out of the sky. First, you can't weigh more than 250 pounds, and second, you can't be taller than 6'5". With FCI safety comes first, so there are no exceptions to these guidelines.

The planes are Extra 300Ls, German-built machines often used by top aerobatic and air show performers. It is as close to a fighter plane as commercially available aircraft are allowed to be; in fact, it even outperforms the F/A-18 Hornet (a standard military machine) on a number of levels. The plane has a roll rate of 360° per second, and it climbs around 3,200 feet per minute. In other words, you will feel the same sensations that you would feel in an actual combat situation, with the G-forces reaching up to five or six in your cockpit. This is the real thing—or as close as a civilian can get.

FCI offers a number of different packages, depending on how much interaction you want to have with the plane, how many people you've got, and, of course, how much you want to pay.

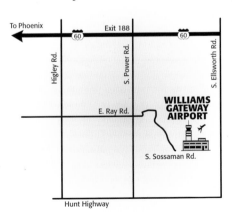

Those of you who have less confidence in your ability than in that of your ten-year seasoned pilot might want to leave the flying to your instructor, thus enjoying the thrill without having to worry about doing much. You'll still be involved, though, as you get to tell your pilot what maneuvers you want to do. You can just sit back and enjoy the ride after giving the order. Unfortunately, these rides are the shortest of the bunch, only lasting around fifteen minutes or a half hour. If you want to log some more airtime, you've got to take the stick yourself. But even at that point, you can still decide just how much of the flying you personally want to do. It'll be worth it to grab the controls for two minutes so that you can later tell your friends that you pulled an inverted flat spin into a hammerhead stall.

Courtesy of Fighter Combat International

Or...for those of you with the desire for the ultimate adventure, there is the Flight of Your Life Super Ride, in which you get to take over the controls completely and have the instructor talk you through various sky moves. This is the package that allows you, someone who's never been closer to a cockpit than the first row of coach, to handle one of the most performance-oriented civilian aircrafts in the sky for close to an hour, which will be plenty of time to tire yourself out as you work to execute the perfect barrel roll.

This adventure is a bit pricey, but the incredible rush is worth every penny. For an activity that seems so initially intimidating, flying under these conditions is actually a lot easier than most people think it will be. Most first-timers are surprised at the skill they show right off the tarmac, and the quickness with which they take complete control of the aircraft. The key is to lose your inhibitions and fears and to push yourself and the plane. It is not every day that you get the chance to fly, so take advantage of this incredible organization, and you'll have a one-of-a-kind memory worth a hundred little bungee jumps, or a million daydreams.

Directions

To get to Williams Gateway Airport from Phoenix, take US-60 east to Power Road (exit 188). DO NOT TAKE THE SOSSAMAN ROAD EXIT OFF US-60. Merge onto and go

Courtesy of Fighter Combat International

right (south) on Power Road for approximately 4.5 miles to the intersection of Power Road and Ray Road. Turn left on Ray Road. Ray Road will veer sharply to the right and become Sossaman Road at this point. Fighter Combat International's facility is on the left side of the road before the Williams Gateway Airport Administration building.

For More Information

Fighter Combat International (see coupon pg 215), Williams Gateway Airport
5803 South Sossaman Rd., Suite 102, Mesa, AZ 85212, 866/359-4273
www.fightercombat.com

Recommended Reading

Franks, Norman. *Aircraft Versus Aircraft: The Illustrated Story of Fighter Pilot Combat From 1914 to the Present Day.* London, England: Grub Street Press, 1999.
Szurovy, Geza. *Basic Aerobatics.* New York, NY: McGraw-Hill Professional Publishing, 1994.
Wagstaff, Patty. *Fire and Air: A Life on the Edge.*
Chicago, IL: Chicago Review Press, 1997.

48 ATV Dune Runners
Hot Springs & Hot Doggers

In the distance, orange flags pop up and down across the horizon, growing closer until you can hear the whiny rumble of the ATVs they are attached to. Then a solo motorcycle spitting sandy rooster tails flies off a mound just several hundred yards away. A pair of sand rails scoot along a ridge before dropping in. You look around…the coast is clear. With a flick of your thumb, suddenly you're speeding through the sand.

The Hot Well Dunes Recreation area is fun. Almost 2,000 acres of open-driving sand dunes provide a playground for all types of vehicles, ranging from motorcycles to ATVs (quads) to sand rails (dune buggies) to 4WD trucks. This incredible area for off-highway vehicle (OHV) enthusiasts is a perfect spot for a weekend escape.

All types of OHVs are permitted to ride anywhere within the fenced boundary, as well as on the existing trails and roads outside of the area. First time visitors should scout the area to get a better idea of where the boundaries are located. With the variety of vehicles using the area, you must keep a careful watch for others. Be especially careful when crossing over dune drop-offs. While flying off a ridge can be a lot of fun, crashing into someone on the other side isn't!

Getting to Arizona's sand dunes is easy. After following the highway from Safford, a gravel road leads the way to the area. RVs and those pulling trailers will find the route very well maintained, but keep watch for the occasional erosion-caused dip. Along the drive, the terrain starts to open up and your excitement will grow. Turning into the area, you'll hear the OHVs ripping around, so be sure to drive slowly on this road.

If you don't own an ATV, several companies offer rentals, but keep in mind that these won't be the most high performance machines; they are better suited for those who just want to give it a try for the weekend. The prices are reasonable, under $100 per machine per day, but a deposit is required. If there are only two of you, you might want to get two quads, but larger groups can share the time on the machines and have a great time. Since the Hot Well Dunes are somewhat isolated, you'll have to transport your rental ATV on a trailer, so you'll need a vehicle with a trailer hitch. If you are a first-time rider and intimidated by the power at the tip of your thumb, the rental companies often offer guided trail rides. Be sure to ask if that interests you.

Upon arrival at the dunes, you need to first pay the daily use fee at the self-service pay station. The fee is $3 per vehicle per day or an annual permit is available for $30 at the Safford Bureau of Land Management office. Of course, if you want to give more, please do! The fees collected go directly back to the site to improve and maintain the access roads, campsites, restroom facilities, hot tubs, picnic areas, and parking.

Hotels are easy to find in nearby Safford, however, camping, which is included in the use fee, is the most popular way to stay. Dozens of established sites are available but fill up quickly, especially on holiday weekends. Your chances of getting a site with a little shade and a picnic

table improve greatly by arriving early. Even if you arrive late, there will be plenty of places to pitch a tent. The area is huge, so you can find a more isolated spot if you desire, and there is also a "family camping" area if you want to stay away from the louder, beer-drinking, bonfire-building, party campers. Overall, the people you'll find here are a fun group.

The facilities are basic, with no electricity, phone, or drinking water, but they do include fire grills and outhouse-style toilet facilities. Fires are allowed in the area, but only in the established campfire rings. If you do plan on having a fire, you must bring your own wood, including kindling, as wood is not available on site.

One of the biggest draws is the natural hot spring, which is channeled into two developed soaking tubs. Riding ATVs is a workout. Your hands and arms always get tired, and if you like to drive more aggressively, your entire body will ache from leaning into the turns. As you push the limits, the occasional fall from the machine can be especially painful. When you're thoroughly fatigued, the best way to ease the aches is to soak away your soreness in the hot spring tubs. The water flowing into the tubs stays around 105 degrees Fahrenheit, which can be quite hot, but also quite refreshing.

The biggest things to remember when heading to the Hot Well Dunes are to bring a form of shade and plenty of drinking water. The existing shade is very sparse so hot and sunny days can be torturous. Helmets, pants, and a long-sleeved shirt are recommended while riding. Be sure to bring a hat and sunscreen. A sun canopy or tarp is a great idea for your campsite. And, as we mentioned before, there are no sources of drinking water nearby, so one gallon per person per day is the minimum, and more is required in hot weather.

Your first time to the dunes can be somewhat intimidating. The area seems immense and after driving around on your quad for only a few minutes, you'll think how easy it would be to get lost. Luckily, the entire area is fenced, but be sure to do some scouting of the boundaries before you let loose; you might not see the fence too easily once you get moving. At the hot spring, the BLM has posted more information including a detailed area map to show you where to go. It might also be a good idea to bring a pin-on bubble compass for when you are driving outside of the fenced boundary to keep your bearings.

After looking at the map, start your adventure at the highest waypoint within the designated riding area. To get there, follow the main road past the campsites and the hot spring, then take a left just before the cattle guard. Try to stay on the main track, but generally just head uphill and you'll find it. The views are far-reaching and give you an idea of the varying terrain. From the top, you'll also see high-performance machines screaming up the sandy incline and racing others. The younger hot dogger crowd calls the peak "Comp Hill" ("comp" is short for "competition"). Old-timers and regulars simply call it the "Big Hill." There is only one large island of brushy vegetation at the top, so expect to see a crowd huddling close together to seek solace from the sun. Sand rails often tote coolers and lawn chairs up the hill for relaxing and enjoying the show.

No special equipment is needed for this escape besides the rental quad. For safety purposes, though, you might want to request a whip. The whip is a tall antenna-like pole with an orange flag at the top. This helps others see you. Paddle tires are popular in the sand, but with the variety of terrain available here, regular ATV tires will work well too. A helmet is highly recommended; besides protecting your head on impact, it also offers sun relief. Goggles are a good idea unless you like a lot of sand in your eyes. When you rent your ATV, be sure to ask for a helmet and goggles as most rental agencies will include both free of charge.

Renting an ATV and heading to the Hot Well Dunes Recreation Area is a wonderful weekend escape. The summer heat is too much for most people, but during the cooler

months, you'll find a fun-loving community of OHV enthusiasts at the area. Riding quads is a very popular activity for all ages; children as young as five or six years old can be found at the dunes. Whatever your skill level and whatever your age, you'll certainly have a blast. Chances are, after a weekend visit to the dunes, you just might be investing in a brand new ATV—quads are highly addictive fun.

Directions

Follow Hwy 70 east from Globe towards Safford. Continue past Safford for 7.3 miles. Turn right (south) on Haekel Road. Follow it for 25 miles. The sign and road for the Hot Well Dunes Recreation Area will be on the left.

Outfitters

ATV's Unlimited (see coupon pg 215), Anywhere Anytime, Greer, AZ, 866/615-1900
Play-Time Sports, ATV Rentals and Tours, Globe, AZ, 866/615-1900, 928/402-9195
Rocco's Racing, Inc. (see coupon pg 215), 2450 E. Bell Road, Phoenix, AZ
602/765-3324, www.roccosracing.com

For More Information

Arizona State Parks, Off Highway Vehicle (OHV) Program, 866/463-6648
www.azohv.com
Safford BLM Office, 711 14th Ave, Safford, AZ 85546, 928/348-4400
http://safford.az.blm.gov

Recommended Reading

Bishop, Christopher. *Chilton's ATV Handbook (Chilton's General Interest Manuals)*. Albany, NY: Delmar Publishers, 1999.
Burch, Monte. *The Field & Stream All-Terrain Vehicle Handbook: The Complete Guide to Owning and Maintaining an ATV*. New York, NY: The Lyons Press, 2001.

Canyon de Chelly
Rock Canyon Ramblings

| Medium |
| $0-$500 |

Unlike the majestic beauty of Sedona's red rocks, the rugged magnificence of the Grand Canyon, or the hidden paradise of Havasu Canyon, much of the far northeast corner of Arizona is relatively flat and dry. Beyond the Painted Desert, the occasional mesa poking out of the wide reaching valleys makes for scenery far less spectacular than in other parts of the Southwest. While the geological processes were creating Arizona's trademark landscapes, the terrain around Chinle, the largest town in the area, appears to have been forgotten. However, one of the main reasons why Chinle is the biggest town is because it's your starting point and gateway to Canyon de Chelly National Monument.

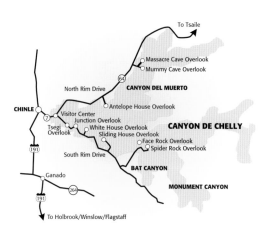

Canyon de Chelly (pronounced "d'shay" from the Navajo word "Tsegi" meaning "rock canyon") is comparatively less tourist-packed than the other more popular areas of the state. Carved from the Colorado Plateau, much of Canyon de Chelly is guarded by sheer cliff walls standing over 1000 feet high. The Monument is actually comprised of multiple canyons, with Canyon del Muerto being the largest. In addition to Canyon de Chelly, smaller canyons like Bat Canyon and Monument Canyon are found in the southern region. Over two million years of water cutting through the sandstone created geological formations so precise that early explorers could be just miles from the rim and not realize the canyons were even there! These deep gorges allowed humans to live uninterrupted in the area for over 5,000 years.

Since entrance to this National Monument is free, one of the easiest and most popular way to access Canyon de Chelly is simply by driving around the rim and stopping at the various lookout points. The North Rim Drive is a 34-mile roundtrip route, which offers three turnoffs leading to various overlooks. The first turnoff leads to the overlook of Antelope House Ruins. Ledge Ruins, Mummy Cave, and Massacre Cave can also be seen from other impressive overlooks. At this last location, visitors can stand at the same spot where, in 1805, a Spanish expedition fired weapons down at a shelter, ultimately killing 115 people. After retracing your route, the South Rim Drive is 37 miles roundtrip and offers seven lookout stops including Tsegi, Junction, White House, Sliding House, Wild Cherry, Face Rock, and Spider Rock. Spider Rock and White House Ruins are the most photographed sites in the Canyon. While enjoying the scenery, be sure to keep an eye on the children. The vertical drops are very dangerous, so always stay on the paths.

Getting off the road and into the Canyon almost always requires hiring an authorized Navajo guide. This ensures the preservation of the 2,700 plus archeological sites that are located in the Canyon. However, the one trail within the National Monument that can be hiked without a guide is the path leading to White House Ruins. At just over a mile each way, the skill and endurance needed for the jaunt is, at most, moderate. The one thing to

Photograph by Ray Bangs

watch, though, is the intense summer heat. Going in the cooler months promises more enjoyable weather for this spectacular hike of terra cotta red rocks leading you into the Canyon. When you get to the actual ruins, don't be disappointed to find that they are fenced off. Many of the petroglyphs and wall paintings are large enough that you can easily see them through the fence, so it is well worth the hike.

If experiencing the awe of these spectacular ruins isn't enough to satisfy you, think about taking a privately guided tour into other parts of the Canyon. Imagine camping near the base of Spider Rock, far below the overlook, and spending the night gazing at the stars. Imagine the excitement of backpacking or riding a horse to get there. Even with minimal horseback experience, the sandy and generally level trails are forgiving and easy for novice equestrians. Although shallow, the water crossings are very exciting. Navajo guides lead hiking and horseback tours to various areas of the National Monument lasting from several hours to multiple days. If walking or going on horseback is not for you, a faster-paced option is also available with the guides taking you through the Canyon in Jeeps and other off-road vehicles. If you own a SUV or 4WD truck, you can save some money by hiring a guide to ride along with you in your own vehicle. Jeep tours usually last just a couple hours, but multiple day adventures can be arranged.

Canyon de Chelly can get quite cold in the winter and the inner canyons can become impassable; however, all you have to do is wear warmer clothing to enjoy the smaller numbers of tourists. Guided tours still operate, but on a sometimes limited basis. Generally, the best time to go is late spring or early summer, but accommodations can fill up rapidly if you are planning anything at the last minute. While the snow often helps create even more dramatic landscapes, the weather might be too cold for staying in a tent. However, if you haven't tried it, spending the night curled up in a toasty sleeping bag with the crisp winter air fogging your breath is always invigorating!

Camping is available on a first-come, first-served basis at the Cottonwood Campground, but reservations are required for group sites of 15 people or more. For those who don't own a four-season tent, the only lodging option within the Monument is at the Thunderbird Lodge, a 72-room motel-style facility reminiscent of older adobe structures.

The cafeteria-style restaurant, which is located in the original trading post (built in 1896), offers both continental and Navajo-style meals seven days a week. Conveniently, the Thunderbird Lodge offers very reasonable, excellent half- and full-day Canyon tours in heavy-duty six-wheel-drive vehicles. Gas, food, and more lodging options can be found in Chinle, two miles from the visitor center.

Both the simple rim tour and the hike to White House Ruins are great introductions to this scaled-down version of the Grand Canyon. Keep in mind that if you want to visit any of the other ruin sites by hiking, horseback riding, or jeep touring, you must hire a guide. These tours can occasionally be full months in advance, and are very popular since the guides can show you other ruins, which are not fenced in and are even more impressive. Additionally, daily hikes led by Rangers are usually available from May to September— be sure to check with the visitor center before and upon arrival for last minute updates. No matter which way you decide to see the Canyon, you will gain invaluable insight into the history and geology of this spiritual place. The whole idea is to become less of a tourist, and instead, more of an historian, a guest, and an explorer…Canyon de Chelly is a great place to start.

Directions
From Flagstaff, follow I-40 east towards Winslow for approximately 140 miles. Signs indicate popular stops, including the Petrified Forest National Park and the Painted Desert. Exit at Chambers and go north on Hwy 191 towards Ganado. In Ganado, US 191 follows AZ Hwy 264 east for six miles. Turn right (north) back on Hwy 191 and drive approximately 30 miles to Chinle. In Chinle, take a right at the stoplight, and follow the signs.

Vehicle Tours
Canyon de Chelly Tours, 928/674-5433, www.canyondechellytours.com
Thunderbird Lodge Canyon Tours (see coupon pg 215), 800/679-2473
    www.tbirdlodge.com
Tsegi Guide Association (tours in your own 4WD vehicle) 928/674-5500
Hiking Tours, Tsegi Guide Association, 520/674-5500
Walk Softly Tours (see coupon pg 217), Scottsdale, Arizona, 480/473-1148
    www.walksoftlytours.com
Horseback Tours, Largo Navajoland Tours, Window Rock, Arizona
    888/726-9084, www.navajolandtours.com

For More Information
Canyon de Chelly National Monument, Chinle, AZ, 928/674-5500
    www.nps.gov/cach

Recommended Reading
Grant, Campbell. *Canyon de Chelly, Its People and Rock Art.*
    Tucson, AZ: University of Arizona Press, 1983.
Noble, David. *Houses beneath the Rock: The Anasazi of Canyon de Chelly and*
    Navajo National Monument. Santa Fe, NM: Ancient City Press, 1993.
Thybony, Scott. *Canyon de Chelly National Monument.*
    Tucson, AZ: Southwest Parks and Monuments Association, 1997.

Humphreys Peak

Conquering the Everest of Arizona

Difficult
$0–$250

Humphreys Peak is Arizona's tallest mountain, standing 12,633 feet above sea level. The difference in elevation is not quite that extreme when hiking, though, as the trail starts at 9,300 feet. Obviously, this is not Mt. Whitney (and only a mid-day shadow of Everest), but for low elevation desert dwellers, Humphreys Peak is a pretty impressive piece of rock.

Of the western highpoints, Humphreys Peak is one of the easiest to hike. During the summer, you can hike the moderate 4.5-mile trail (one-way) from the lower Arizona Snowbowl parking lot to the summit in under three hours. There's no hurry, however, and since this has already become a day trip, you might as well take your time and not suffer the effects of altitude and exhaustion. If you prefer a slower pace, a more realistic goal is four to six hours. Splitting the trip in half by camping is also popular in the warmer months. Dump several feet of snow into the equation and things get really tough. Make sure you're ready for this challenge.

Whether you do it in one day or not, keep in mind that you are ascending more than 3000 vertical feet, and if you are arriving from a lower elevation area like Phoenix, Acute Mountain Sickness (AMS) can occur. If you suffer from two or three of the seven warning signs of AMS (headache, nausea or vomiting, sleep disturbance, dizziness, shortness of breath, loss of appetite, and fatigue), don't question—just descend. Complications arising from altitude can kill you! According to the University of Colorado Health Sciences Center, around one in four will suffer some AMS symptoms when reaching 8,000 feet. With higher elevations, the risk grows higher. Symptoms can last for several days after the onset, and the onset may even be delayed.

As with all hikes above timberline, certain precautions apply in addition to elevation.

Photograph by Tom Bean

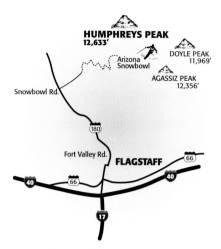

HUMPHREYS PEAK
12,633'

DOYLE PEAK
11,969'

Arizona
Snowbowl

AGASSIZ PEAK
12,356'

Snowbowl Rd.

180

Fort Valley Rd.
FLAGSTAFF
66

40
66
40

17

Since it can snow and rain any month of the year, bring warm clothes and enough high-energy food to fuel your body. While climbing Humphreys Peak, you will be following an exposed ridge where heavy winds year round can make things chilly. Get an early start, especially during the summer monsoon season so that afternoon thunderstorms can be avoided, and definitely avoid the ridge during lightning storms. Additionally, this is NOT the trail to hike in shorts and a t-shirt without bringing any extra gear. Adequate food, water, and warm clothing are essentials even for a summer trip. The weather in the mountains changes quickly.

Once you've reached the summit in the warmer months, you might start thinking about mountaineering in the winter. If visions of crampons and ice axes creep into your mind and you dream of someday climbing the world's tallest peaks, remember that you have to start somewhere. In the winter, with hardly a twist of your imagination and your nearly frozen toes, Humphreys Peak seems to be right out of Alaska's Brooks Range.

One unique aspect of Humphreys Peak is that the trail follows a long ridge where you're unprotected from the forceful gales. Decked out in full gear, this is a spectacular experience, but it can be frightening, too. The summit log is full of stories about people being forced to walk on all fours because of the 50+ mph winds whipping across the ridge. Of course, the flip side is that on a clear day, you can see for more than a hundred miles. Jaw-dropping views of the North Rim of the Grand Canyon, the Painted Desert, and the Mogollon Rim await those who drag themselves all the way to the top. Quite close by is the state's second tallest mountain, 12,356-foot Agassiz Peak, and to the east of that, 11,969-foot Fremont Peak, both of which also offer amazing views.

Humphreys Peak and the rest of the San Francisco Peaks are the remains of dormant volcanoes that erupted thousands of years ago. Natural (and wooden wilderness) signs show that virtually all the peaks you see from the trail are volcanic. The cinder base of the last mile of this climb guarantees uneven footing and regular loss of the trail. It's important to stay on the trail as much as possible to prevent damaging Arizona's only tundra, which hosts the small, endangered San Francisco groundsel found nowhere else in the world. Be certain to keep on the lookout for this miniature sunflower, and don't step on it!

Choosing your trip dates too far in advance leaves the weather up to chance. December to March are the best months for winter climbing, but remember that a fresh snow in excess of a foot can severely hinder and possibly halt your summit attempt. Snowshoes are required equipment. The fresh powder, although beautiful, can also mean increased avalanche danger. Calling the Ranger Station to check conditions on the morning of your hike is highly recommended.

There are two options for the winter ascent, both of which can be quite uncomfortable without the proper gear. Your first choice is to bring equipment to camp just below the treeline. Even protected by the trees and the mountain, winds can still blow fierce all night and drop air temperatures well below freezing. Sleeping bags and tents designed to perform in the extreme cold weather are required. If you can stand poking your head out of the tent, check out the stars in the night sky, which will be especially bright since tight restrictions on light pollution are in place due to the nearby Lowell Peak Observatory.

The second type of ascent is a quick, one-day up and down. Keep the backpack light but check your packing list several times. Insulated mountaineering boots fitted with crampons are a must, and don't forget the ice axe and ski poles.

The group leader may have a moderate amount of trail breaking to do, but generally the route is relatively tame. Stretches of consolidated hardpack are easy to find, especially if it has not snowed in some time. The last section to the summit following along the exposed ridge can be the most grueling part of the climb. The three false summits you have to cross are nothing like the false summits on Colorado's 14ers, but tired muscles and a tired spirit can make that last push especially challenging. Hope for light winds and be sure to pack along a wind-breaking parka, mittens, and a facemask.

After making a couple of cell phone calls from the summit, which although popular is definitely an etiquette no-no if others are on the peak, the trip down usually goes quickly. Whether using snowshoes or regular boots and crampons, you can plunge-step down the slope. Don't go too fast, though, because the angles are somewhat deceptive and you might have a tumble or two. The clamber down takes less than half the time of the ascent.

Alpine mountaineering is a spiritual and life-changing pursuit. The mountains push you to your limits and beyond, so the entire key to success is your endurance and mental fortitude. You just have to keep putting one foot in front of the other, and eventually, you'll make it to the top. Humphreys Peak, although half the size of the Himalayan Mountains, is a challenging and out-of-the ordinary escape from the sun-baked desert. Most people who start climbing find that they love it, stick with it, and soon enough, usually find themselves atop some exotic peak in some distant country. And, in the words of Chuck Pratt, "…writing about climbing is boring. I would rather go climbing." Winter is always just around the corner.

Directions

From Phoenix follow I-17 north to the I-17/I-40 Junction. Keep heading north 1.8 miles on Milton Rd. (I-17 becomes Milton Rd. and Milton Rd. becomes Route 66) Proceed under the train bridge and follow the curve towards the east. At the first stoplight, turn left onto Humphreys St. (Hwy 180). Proceed on Humphreys for .6 miles to Ft. Valley Rd. Turn left on Ft. Valley Rd. (Hwy 180) and proceed 6.8 miles to the Arizona Snowbowl road turn off. Ski Lift Lodge is located at this intersection. Turn right onto Snowbowl Rd. and proceed approximately 7 miles up the mountain to the lower lodge. Please drive carefully on Snowbowl Rd. as there are steep grades, winding roads, and wildlife in this area. Park in the lot on the left side and follow the signs to the trailhead.

For More Information

Coconino National Forest, Peaks Ranger Station, 5075 N. Highway 89, Flagstaff, AZ
928/526-0866, www.fs.fed.us/r3/coconino

Recommended Reading

Gorman, Stephen. *Winter Camping.*
    Boston, MA: Appalachian Mountain Club, 1999.
Graydon, Don. *Mountaineering: The Freedom of the Hills.*
    Seattle, WA: The Mountaineers, 1997.
Rutstrum, Calvin. *Paradise Below Zero: The Classic Guide to Winter Camping.*
    Minneapolis, MN: University of Minnesota Press, 2000.

Survival School
Exploring Your Wild Side

You're looking up through evergreens, watching the sun set through the maze of branches above you. Rays dance across a deep, velvety carpet of needles and burn the blue sky into yellows and oranges. It's still early—won't be dark for another hour or so—but your stomach is impatient for the pot of stew now boiling away over your fire. You're a little tired, but not too bad, as you didn't carry very much on the way in.

Not having that tent to lug around is liberating, you think, even if building the shelter took up a little more time than you would have liked. You sit down by the fire, the one you made without so much as a match, and know that now, on your second day, you would be able to get by even without your guide. You feel self-sufficient, more so than you ever have before, able to take care of yourself in the outdoors. It's a nice feeling, a confident one. When the stew's done, you pick up your stick-spoon, the small flat utensil you carved, and dig in.

This scene isn't one you'll experience if you're on a traditional camping trip. But if you're enrolled in one of Arizona's survival schools, learning to brave the deserts and wilderness with nothing but a blanket, some food, a knife, and a cooking pot, you will feel an amazing sense of freedom that few people get to experience. You'll sleep in shelters you build yourself, forage for edible plants, create fire with sticks and stones, and generally experience the world as our ancestors did. You'll even learn how to navigate the wilderness without a map, using the clues nature provides.

In all, survival school is both a great way to gain new skills and augment the ones that you may, if you hike and camp frequently, already have. Imagine not needing your water-

proof matches; being able to carry half as much food in your pack, because you feel comfortable foraging the rest; or even leaving the tent at home all the time, because you can build a shelter more sturdy than nylon. You may not get to that point after one session of survival school, but if you make it a regular part of your outdoor adventuring, you just might be able to lighten that backpack by quite a few pounds.

Survival schools are versatile institutions that offer a huge variety of emphases. Nature education, which includes learning what berries to eat, what plants to stay away from, and where to find tasty edible insects, is a big part of what you will learn. Primitive technology training, in which students learn to make bows, arrows, snares, and stone tools, is also quite popular. Wilderness living skills, which are basic necessities like fire-making and how to find water, round out the curriculum.

In general, a good survival class will teach a little bit of all things, at least enough to get by. Most schools offer classes of differing lengths, from single-day seminars to marathon month-long sessions. For beginners, anything from a one-day class to three

Courtesy of Ancient Pathways

days in the bush will provide a great introduction to wilderness survival and provide plenty of opportunities to pick up skills you'll use on the trail in the future.

Survival schools also vary a great deal in their philosophies. Some take a very reverent approach to survival, seeing it as a hearkening call back to a simpler, yet more difficult time; others treat survival as something of a sport, a kind of extreme camping; still others take a goal-oriented path fit for corporate escapes and team-building exercises. When you call to make reservations, you will already know what kind of organization you'll be dealing with; it's usually apparent from their literature, web sites, etc. In any case, keep this difference in styles foremost in your mind, as you'll want to match your tempera-ment to that of the survival school you choose.

Arizona is a great place for survival training, simply because the state offers so many different kinds of terrain in a relatively small area. Survival schools operate all over the state, from Flagstaff to the southeastern Chiricahua Mountains. Ancient Pathways, a survival school based in Flagstaff, boasts that its participants get to experience terrain from the Sonoran desert to alpine mountains. They offer the variety of classes outlined above, with an emphasis on natural science and the Native American history of the area. Their specialty is the three- to five-day wilderness experience, in which students go into the wild to learn and apply new skills. Ancient Pathways also offers a variety of day classes that teach basic and more advanced skills such as fire by friction, plant identification, knife use, and animal behavior.

The Ability School, based in Phoenix, offers one-day to one-week courses, specializing in desert survival and self-reliance. Still another, Cody Lundin's Aboriginal Living Skills School, provides a class designed to show those taking on the wilderness with modern gear what to do if that gear should fail or be lost. Obviously, each school has a very different slate of classes, and among them, you're sure to find just the right class for you.

Another good thing about this adventure is that you get a lot of activity for your money. Ancient Pathway's three-day class costs only $225 per person, and this price includes all instruction, food, and the various tools you'll make during your primitive technology training. Since you won't have any shelter to pay for, it makes for a fairly inexpensive three days!

If you take a survival class and enjoy it, there are plenty of opportunities to hone your skills under more extreme circumstances. Ancient Pathways offers a two-day "knife only" class to those people who have had previous survival training. Boulder Outdoor Survival School (BOSS) offers trips in southern Utah of up to twenty-eight days long that really put you out there. "Leaving the high tech modern world behind, you explore the desert washes and mountain trails with little more than a knife, a water bottle, a blanket, and a poncho."

Whoa.

Of course, a whole new level of fitness, commitment, and time is necessary for an adventure such as this. In the meantime, though, you can sharpen your skills for a few days at a time and finally learn what those little red berries taste like.

Directions

Call your local outfitter for directions.

Outfitters

Ability (see coupon pg 217), Phoenix, AZ, 602/485-8687, www.abilitywilderness.com
Aboriginal Living Skills School, Prescott, AZ, 928/636-8384, www.alssadventures.com
Ancient Pathways (see coupon pg 217), Flagstaff, AZ, 928/774-7522, www.apathways.com
Boulder Outdoor Survival School, 800/335-7404, www.boss-inc.com
Trail Blazers Adventures (see coupon pg 217), Greer, AZ, 866/615-1900

Recommended Reading

Alloway, David. *Desert Survival Skills*. Austin, TX: University of Texas Press, 2000.
Swarthout, Glendon F. & Swarthout, Kathryn. *Whichaway*.
    Flagstaff, AZ: Rising Moon, 1997.
Wiseman, John. *The SAS Survival Handbook: How to Survive in the Wild, in Any
    Climate, on Land, or at Sea*. New York, NY: Harper Collins Publishing Ltd, 1999.

Dog Sledding

Are We Still in Arizona, Toto?

**Difficult
$100-$500**

We were quickly approaching Don's Cabin, and I felt a pang of disappointment. The running had been good today, and the dogs still looked healthy and strong. The weather was cold and crisp, but not windy. I debated whether to stop. My plan was not to, but I didn't want to push the team too hard. I said nothing and let Raja decide. He was a good lead dog… smart, fast, and confident. I smiled when he didn't even look towards the rickety shelter. We were on our way! Only 54 more miles to Iditarod and 600 to Nome. We'll reach the halfway point tomorrow!

If this vision seems more like something out of a Jack London novel than an Arizona activity, you couldn't be more wrong. For most people, the sun-baked desert, saguaros, and scorching sand sum up our state. But once you escape the Sonoran desert, Arizona has six more ecological zones with dramatically different landscapes, plants, and animals. And, as the ecological zones change, so do the outdoor activities. Mountain biking and hiking are two likely Arizona activities, while whitewater rafting and kayaking are also popular. Most people have even heard about downhill skiing and snowboarding up in the colder areas. But whether you believe it or not, the idea of dog sledding in Arizona is not too-far fetched.

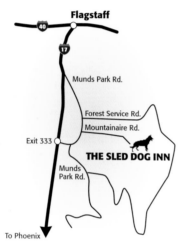

When you mention dog sledding, the picture most people conjure up is of the famous Iditarod race in Alaska. Known as the "Last Great Race," the 1,049-mile (plus a few miles for fun) annual trek covers some of the earth's coldest and toughest terrain. This race draws thousands of spectators each year, and as the sport's popularity continues to grow, so does its leisure appeal. If you're one of the many observers who get hooked on the sport after having seen a race, you can still get the experience of dog sledding with one of at least three dozen top-notch outfitters, who'll all be actively competing for your tourism dollars.

But you're wondering what all this has to do with Arizona, right?

Just outside of Flagstaff, a small bed and breakfast offers one of Arizona's most unique and uncharacteristic winter activities, dog sledding. Obviously, successful dog sledding all depends on the snow conditions, but even in the driest winters, northern Arizona usually gets a few hefty powder days. With enough snow, the Sled Dog Inn offers exciting adventures from early January to the middle of March.

In the course of just a few days, you can learn the basic skills and techniques to get you started and on your way to competing in the Iditarod. Even if you never make it to the big race, though, you can still experience (on a much smaller scale) what the competitors go through and how they feel. The fastest finishers complete the Iditarod course in less than 10 days, sleeping as little as three or four hours a night, and being subjected to -40° F temperatures. At the Sled Dog Inn, you can mush for the day and then return to the Inn for some heavy-duty hot tubbing.

Photograph by Peter Noebel

Photograph by Peter Noebel

In addition to dog sledding, another popular sport called "ski joring" is available to try. Instead of standing on the sled with a team of dogs, you become the sled. With cross-country skies on your feet and one or sometimes two dogs strapped to your waist, the challenge is just trying to stay upright as the dogs pull you across the snow. Although ski jorers claim it's fun and easy "once you get the hang of it," this could definitely be classified as an extreme sport. The real frustration is trying to stop. Since the dogs love to run and keep on running, the joke in the mushing community is that ski jorers use their face for a brake!

The dogs are incredibly strong and intelligent. They respond quickly to an assertive and confident musher. Questioning yourself makes the dogs question you, which although okay at the Sled Dog Inn, could be dangerous if you ever get into bigger backcountry experiences. Reservations are required for dog sledding and ski joring, and is of course dependant on the weather. The minimum age is 16 and you need at least two people to go. Neither of you can weigh less than 95 pounds or more than 220 pounds.

The Sled Dog Inn offers comfortable accommodations well outside the hustle and bustle of downtown Flagstaff. The sunken living room downstairs features a cozy rock fireplace, and the European-style cedar sauna is the perfect way to fend off the winter chills. And on the lighter snow days, all guests are free to pick from the stable of mountain bikes and pedal off into the bordering National Forest. Keep in mind, however, that mountain biking on ice and snow present their own challenges!

So when you are looking for an atypical Arizona adventure, or if you just sadly celebrated your first holiday season sans snow, dog sledding could be just for you. Soon enough, you'll be booking a flight to Alaska and signing up for the Iditarod. Happy Mushing!

Directions

From Phoenix head north on I-17 to exit 333 (Kachina Blvd/Mountainaire Rd.). From the Exit go east (right) on Mountainaire Rd. for 1.3 miles, passing 3 houses on your right. At 1.3 miles turn right onto the Sled Dog Inn driveway. Check in at the main entrance.

For More Information

The Sled Dog Inn Bed & Breakfast , 10155 Mountainaire Rd. , Flagstaff, AZ 86001
800/754-0664, www.sleddoginn.com

Recommended Reading

Kreissman, Bern. *The Complete Winter Sports Safety Manual.*
Helena, MT: Falcon Publishing, 1997.
O'Donoghue, Brian. *Honest Dogs: A Story of Triumph and Regret from the World's Greatest Sled Dog Race.* Kenmore, WA: Epicenter Press, 1999.

RAY BANGS moved to Arizona in 1995, but has already seen more of the state than most lifelong residents. He spends nearly every weekend in the great outdoors pursuing a variety of activities such as skiing, hiking, SCUBA diving, and camping. He is the publisher of AZExplorer.com and *Arizona Explorer Magazine*. Ray lives in Tempe.

CHRIS BECKER has lived in Arizona for four years. Although he is a relative newcomer to outdoor adventure, he is committed to learning all he can about Arizona, while discovering first-hand its many natural wonders. He works as an editor for *Arizona Explorer Magazine* and *Hayden's Ferry Review*. Chris lives in Tempe with his wife, Danielle.